THE
RUM COCKTAIL GUIDE

THE RUM COCKTAIL GUIDE

coladas & daiquiris

== Steve Quirk ==

CONTENTS

Introduction 7

Colada Cocktails 21

Daiquiri Cocktails 53

Glossary 136

Index 140

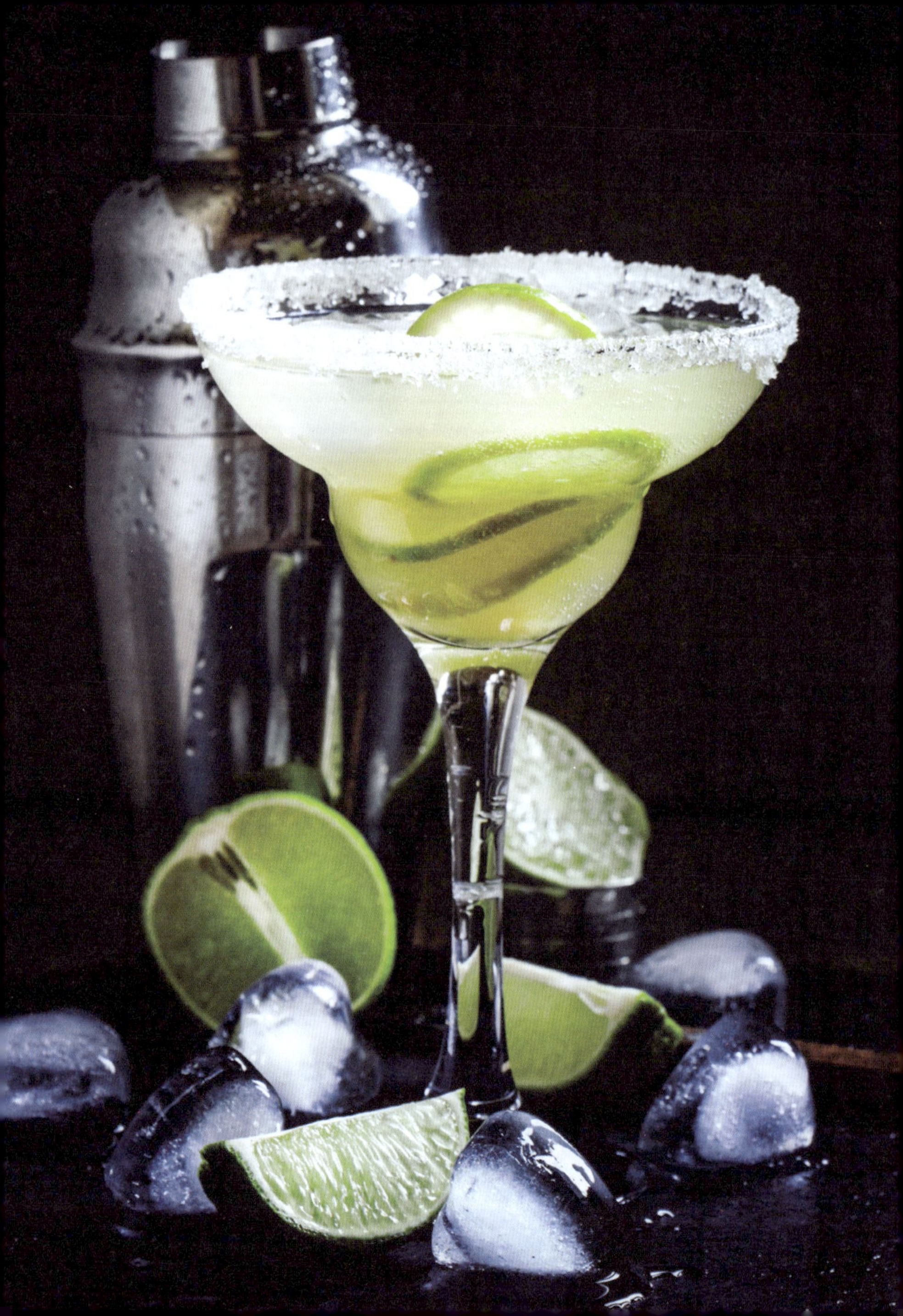

Introduction

Cocktails are believed to have originated in America and are now so popular worldwide that there is a cocktail to satisfy every occasion and palate. This book provides an extensive range of 60 colada and daiquiri cocktails from basic mixers through to exotic creations, demonstrating that there is nothing complicated about preparing a colada or daiquiri cocktail. Each recipe is provided with clear and uncomplicated directions, ensuring that those without previous experience can create a colada or daiquiri cocktail with ease.

Approximate % alcohol volume (% alc/vol) content has been calculated and supplied for each drink in this book, as well as how many standard drinks each contains.

These calculations are based on information obtained that is believed to be accurate and reliable, although they cannot be guaranteed due to % alc/vol variations between the different brands of spirits and liqueurs. These calculations should only be used as a guide.

The % alc/vol for all spirits and liqueurs required for drinks contained within this book are provided in the glossary – if unsure then compare your spirits and liqueurs with the % alc/vol provided in the glossary.

◆ CONSTRUCTING A COCKTAIL ◆

Stirring – Where ingredients are required to be stirred, half-fill a mixing glass with ice and pour the ingredients over the ice. Stir and strain into chosen glass. Usually ingredients that mix easily together are prepared in this manner.

Shaking – When ingredients require shaking, half-fill a cocktail shaker with ice, and then pour the ingredients into the shaker over ice. This will chill the ingredients quicker than pouring the ingredients into the shaker before ice. Avoid over-filling your shaker – leave room for shaking. To shake, stand still and shake vigorously for about ten seconds, strain into your chosen glass and serve or garnish. The majority of cocktail shakers have a strainer; if yours does not then you can use a Hawthorn strainer. Effervescent drinks should never be shaken in a cocktail shaker. Rinse the shaker out thoroughly after each use and dry with a clean lint-free cloth. This will ensure that your drinks only have in them what they are supposed to and will not distort the flavor of the next drink that you prepare.

Blending – When a blender is required, only use cracked or crushed ice in suitable blenders and blend until ingredients are evenly mixed.

◆ USEFUL TIPS ◆

Sugar syrup – To make sugar syrup, bring one cup of ordinary white sugar with one cup of water almost to the boil in a small saucepan stirring continuously and simmer until the sugar is completely dissolved. Remove from heat and allow to cool. Once cool, pour into a resealable container or a corked bottle and store in the refrigerator or behind your bar for regular use. This syrup will now last indefinitely.

Sweet & sour mix – To make sweet & sour mix bring one cup of sugar syrup to the simmer then add ½ cup fresh lemon juice and ½ cup fresh lime juice. Simmer till well mixed stirring frequently, then remove from heat and allow to cool. Once cool, pour into a resealable container or corked bottle and store in refrigerator for up to ten days. Sweet & sour mix is also refered to as sour mix or bar mix.

To chill a glass – Glasses can be chilled by placing them in a refrigerator or by placing ice cubes into the glasses while drinks are being prepared. Discard these ice cubes before pouring unless otherwise instructed.

Fruit, peels and juices – Fruit slices and pieces will keep fresher and longer if covered with a damp clean linen cloth and refrigerated. Where citrus peel is required, cut the peel into required sizes and shave away the white membrane. Fruit and peels should be the last ingredient added to a cocktail (garnish). When juices are required remember – fresh is best. When using canned fruit and/or juices, transfer the cans' contents into appropriate resealable containers and refrigerate.

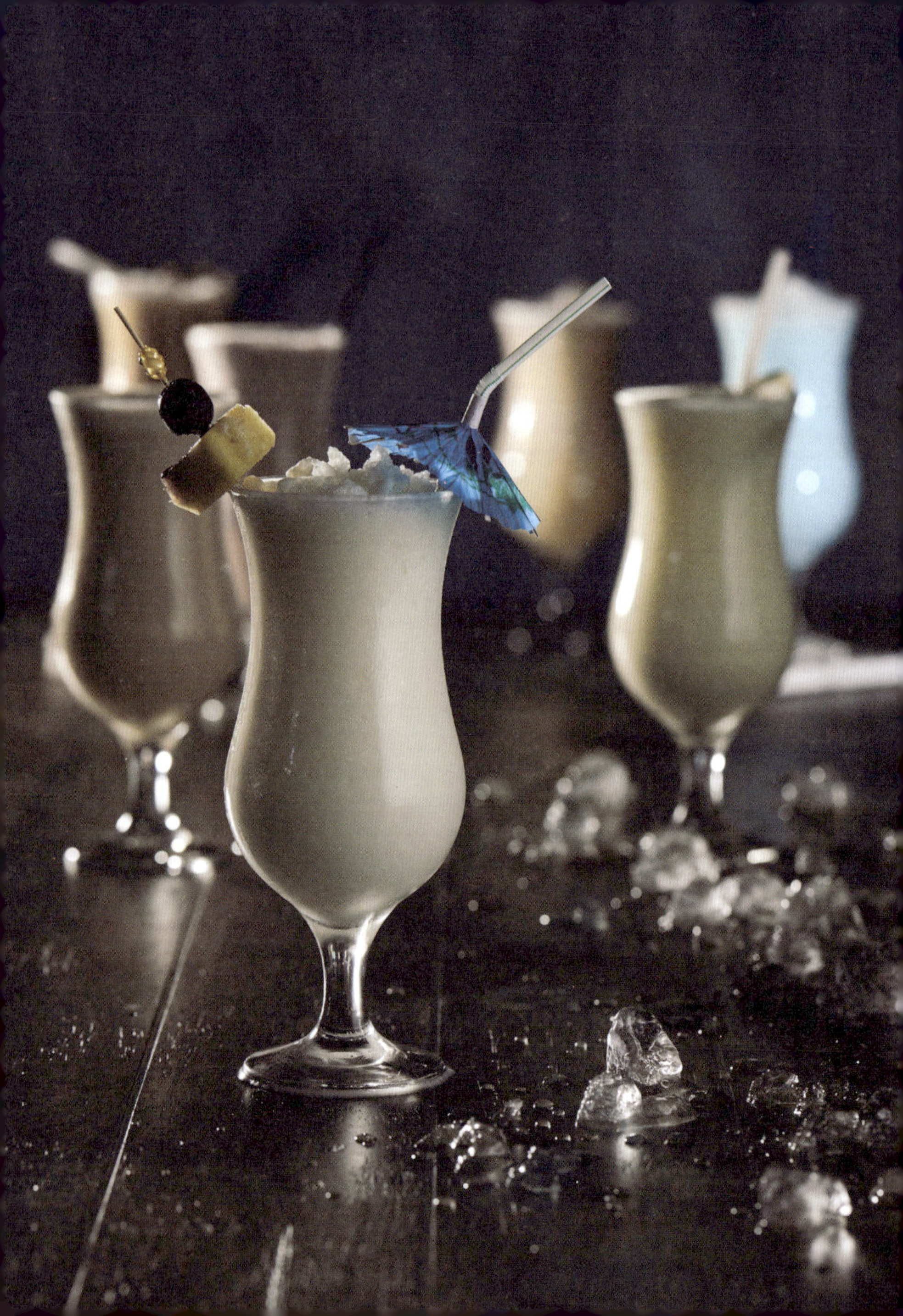

Ice – It is important to maintain a well-stocked clean ice supply, as most colada and daiquiri cocktails require ice during construction. To obtain crushed ice if you do not have access to an ice-crushing machine, place required ice onto a clean linen cloth and fold up. Place ice-filled cloth onto a hard surface and smash with a mallet (not a bottle).

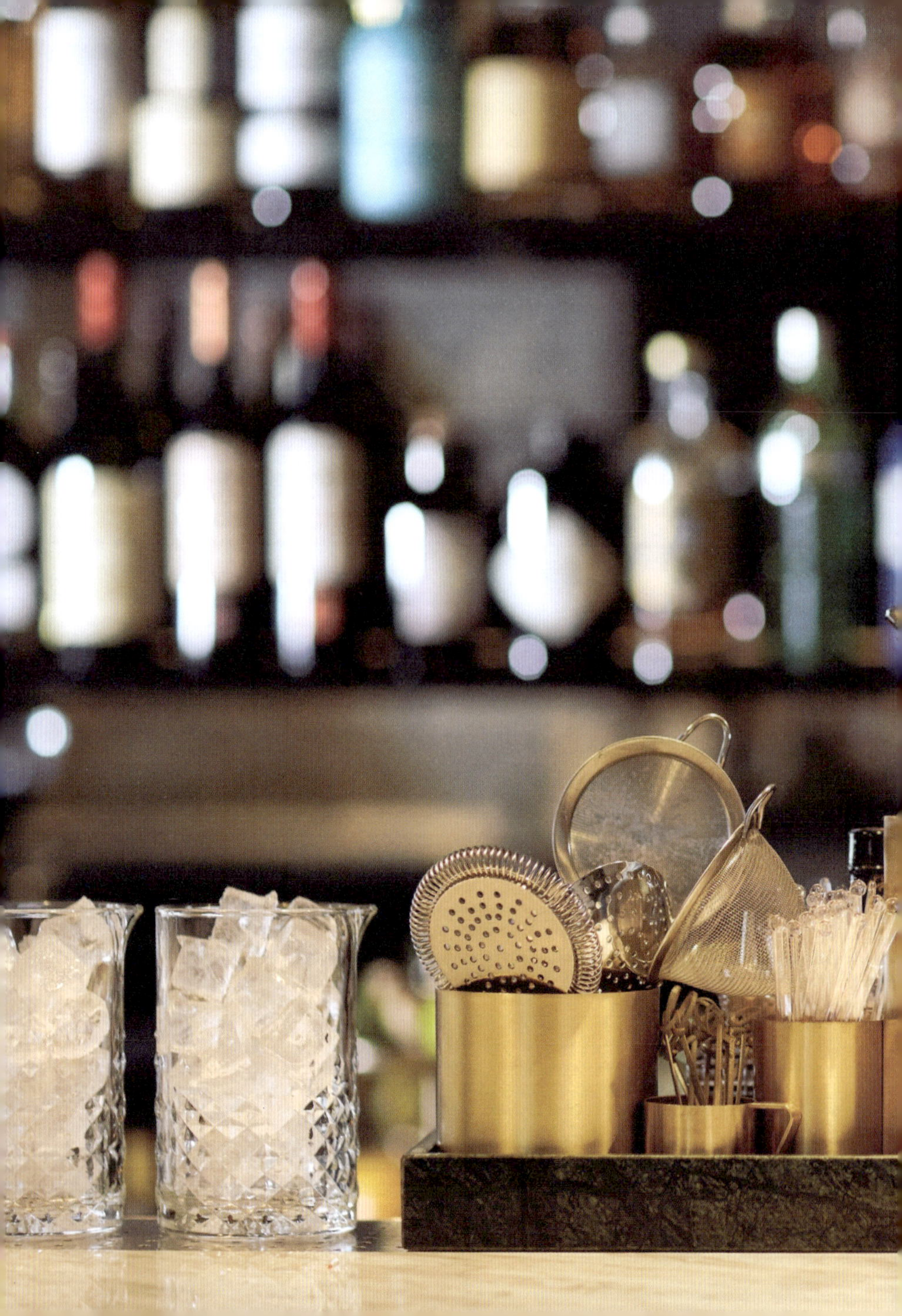

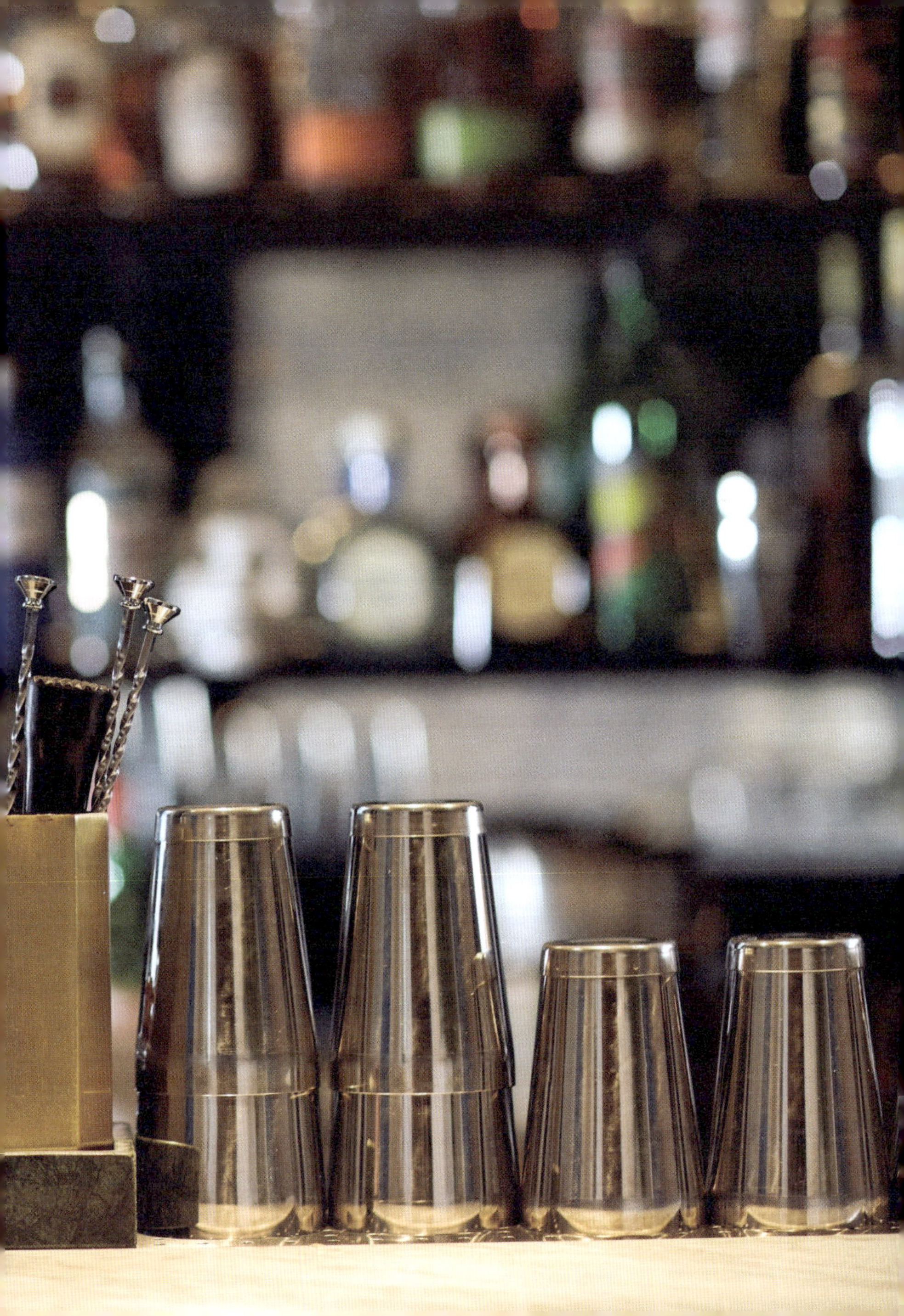

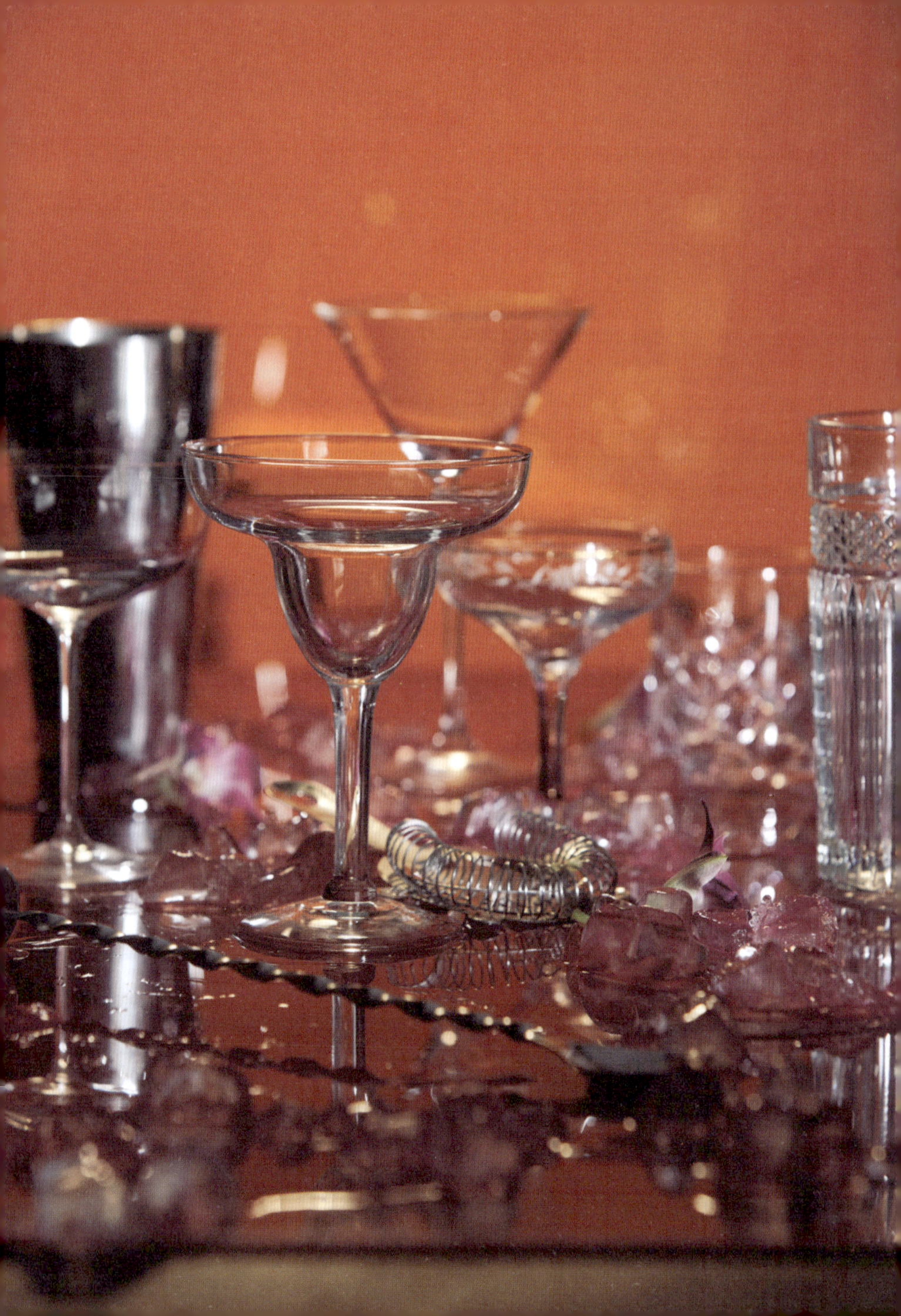

◆ GLASSWARE ◆

Glasses come in a wide variety of shapes and sizes and range in value depending upon the quality of glass. When washing glasses, use hot water without detergent to avoid distorting the flavor of a drink. Only wash one glass at a time and dry with a clean lint-free cloth. Before using a glass, give it a quick polish with a glass cloth and check glass for chips and/or cracks. When handling glassware, hold glasses by their base or stem as this will avoid finger marks around the rim of glass, thus maintaining a high polish.

The following is a compiled list of glassware required for colada and daiquiri cocktails within this publication, although for the home bar an extensive range of glassware is not always necessary. As an example, a wine glass could be used as a cocktail glass.

- **Champagne Saucer** 140 ml (4⅔ fl oz) – 180 ml (6 fl oz)
- **Cocktail** 90 ml (3 fl oz) – 140 ml (4⅔ fl oz)
- **Goblet** 140 ml (4⅔ fl oz) – 285 ml (9½ fl oz)
- **Hurricane** 230 ml (7⅔ fl oz) – 650 ml (21⅔ fl oz)
- **Margarita** 260 ml (8⅔ fl oz)

MEASURES
1 dash 1 ml (1/30 fl oz)
1 teaspoon 5 ml (⅙ fl oz)
1 cup 250 ml (8⅓ fl oz)

COMMON INGREDIENTS FOR COLADA AND DAIQUIRICOCKTAILS

Spirits
Bacardi
Light Rum
Sherry

Liqueurs
Midori
Banana Liqueur
Strawberry Liqueur
Cointreau
Curaçao

COMMON MIXERS

- Apple Juice
- Pineapple Juice
- Coconut Cream
- Sweet & Sour Mix
- Cream
- Lemon Juice
- Lime Juice
- Orange Juice
- Eggs

GARNISHES AND ADDITIVES

- Sugar
- Bananas
- Kiwi Fruit
- Peaches
- Lemons
- Limes
- Strawberries
- Sprigs of Mint
- Maraschino Cherries
- Oranges
- Pineapple

◆ HOSTING A COLADA AND DAIQUIRI COCKTAIL PARTY ◆

To be the host of a party can be stressful if you are not properly prepared. Here are some helpful hints to ensure that you and your guests enjoy the occasion.

It is advisable to pre-cut your fruit for garnishes and wrap them in plastic or place a clean damp linen cloth over them and refrigerate until required. Juices should be squeezed and/or removed from tin cans. Pour juices into resealable containers and refrigerate. Make up a bowl of sugar syrup as described under useful tips, this will save you from having to dissolve sugar when preparing large quantities of drinks. Keep a glass of water on your bar for rinsing instruments such as spoons and stirrers. If your washing machine is in close proximity to your bar or kitchen, it can be used to fill with clean fresh ice. This will keep the ice chilled and will be less mess to clean up during and after your party.

If you find yourself hosting a large party, it is an idea to make yourself a checklist of what you require and what must be completed. Once your list is all checked off, you should then be able to sit down and relax before your home is invaded by guests. Then you can enjoy delectable colada and daiquiri cocktails with family and friends without the stress of hosting the occasion.

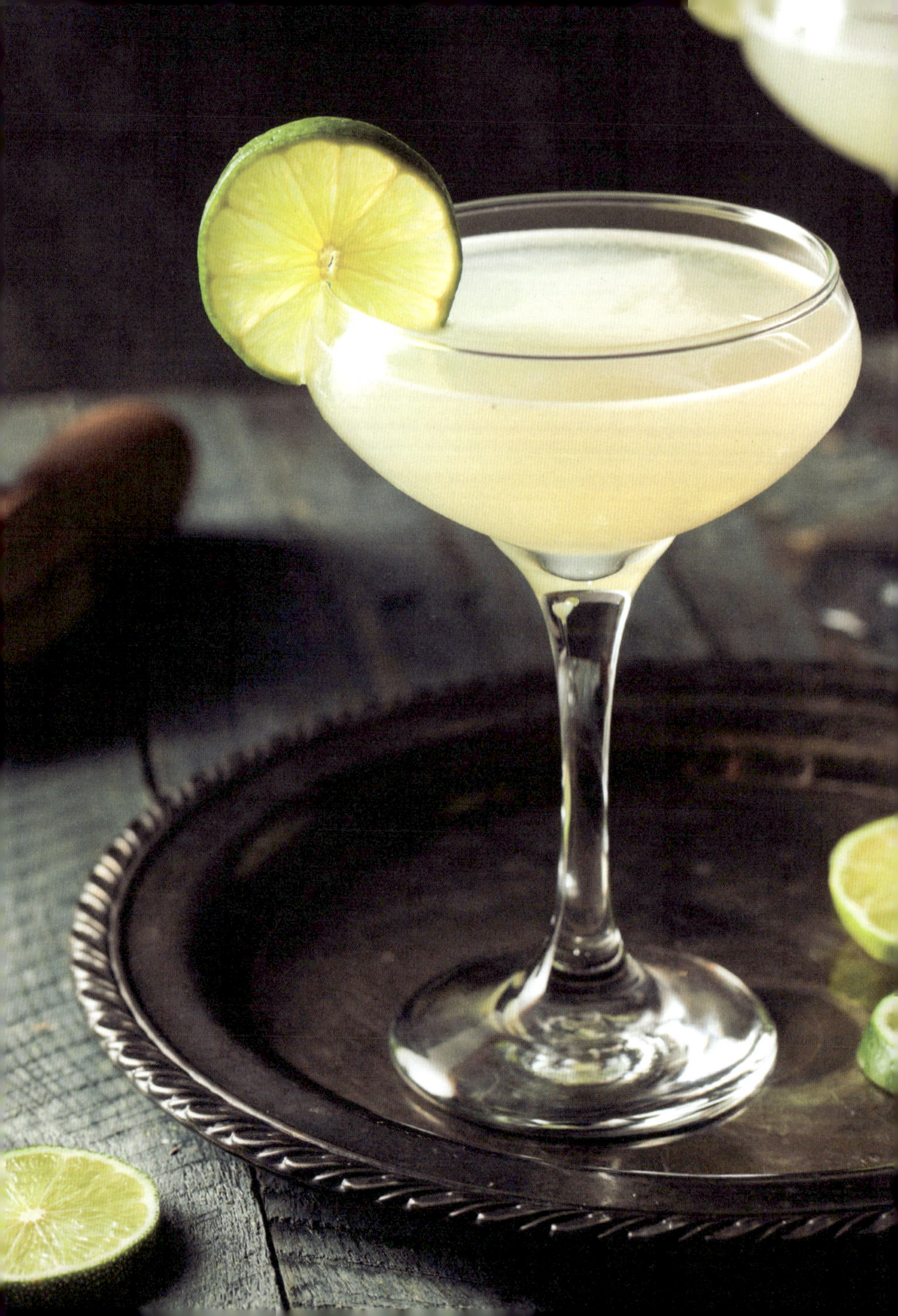

◆ CORDIALS AND LIQUEURS ◆

Cordials and liqueurs are alcohol-based with herbs, aromatic plants, essences, juices, beans, nuts, dairy products, sweeteners and colors which are infused in the spirit by the process of steeping and distillation.

Traditionally, cordials and liqueurs were created for medicinal purposes as a cure for all types of ills. Creating cordials and liqueurs hundreds of years ago meant that people would gather herbs, fruits and plants from their gardens and then added them with sugar to liquors such as gin and brandy. Today cordials and liqueurs are produced by distilling companies worldwide. It would not be possible to list all cordials and liqueurs that are being produced or available. A list has been provided of the main ones that are required for colada and daiquiri cocktails in the introduction of this book.

Cordials and liqueurs are essential ingredients in a vast variety of colada and daiquiri cocktails.

♦♦♦

The history of the colada began with the creation of the Piña Colada in 1954. The Piña Colada was created by Ramon "Monchito" Marrero whilst he was a bartender at the Caribe Hilton Hotel in San Juan, Puerto Rico. Ramon Marrero wanted to combine the flavors of Puerto Rico into a drink.

Piña Colada was declared to be the national drink of Puerto Rico in 1978. Piña Colada translates in Spanish as "strained pineapple". Today there are many varieties of colada cocktails, with the majority containing light rum, coconut cream and pineapple juice which are served in hurricane glasses.

♦♦♦

Colada

COCKTAILS

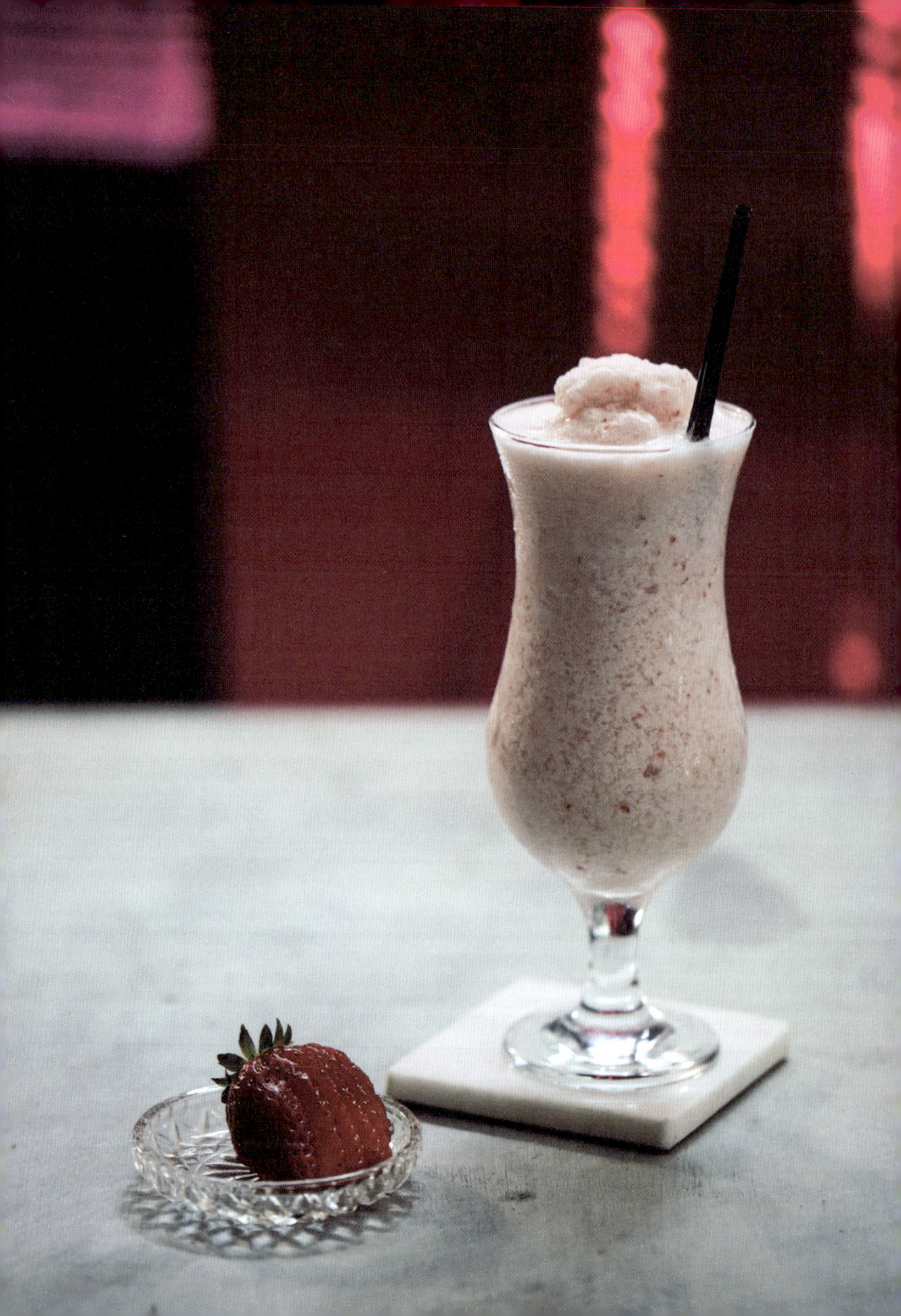

STRAWBERRY COLADA

9.4% alc/vol
1.7 standard drinks

38 ml (1¼ fl oz) light rum
38 ml (1¼ fl oz) strawberry liqueur
90 ml (3 fl oz) pineapple juice
40 ml (1⅓ fl oz) coconut cream (chilled)
1 teaspoon thick cream (chilled)
2 fresh strawberries (diced)

Pour rum, liqueur, juice and creams into a blender over a large amount of crushed ice then add diced strawberries. Blend until slushy and pour into a chilled hurricane glass. Garnish with fresh fruit and then serve with a straw.

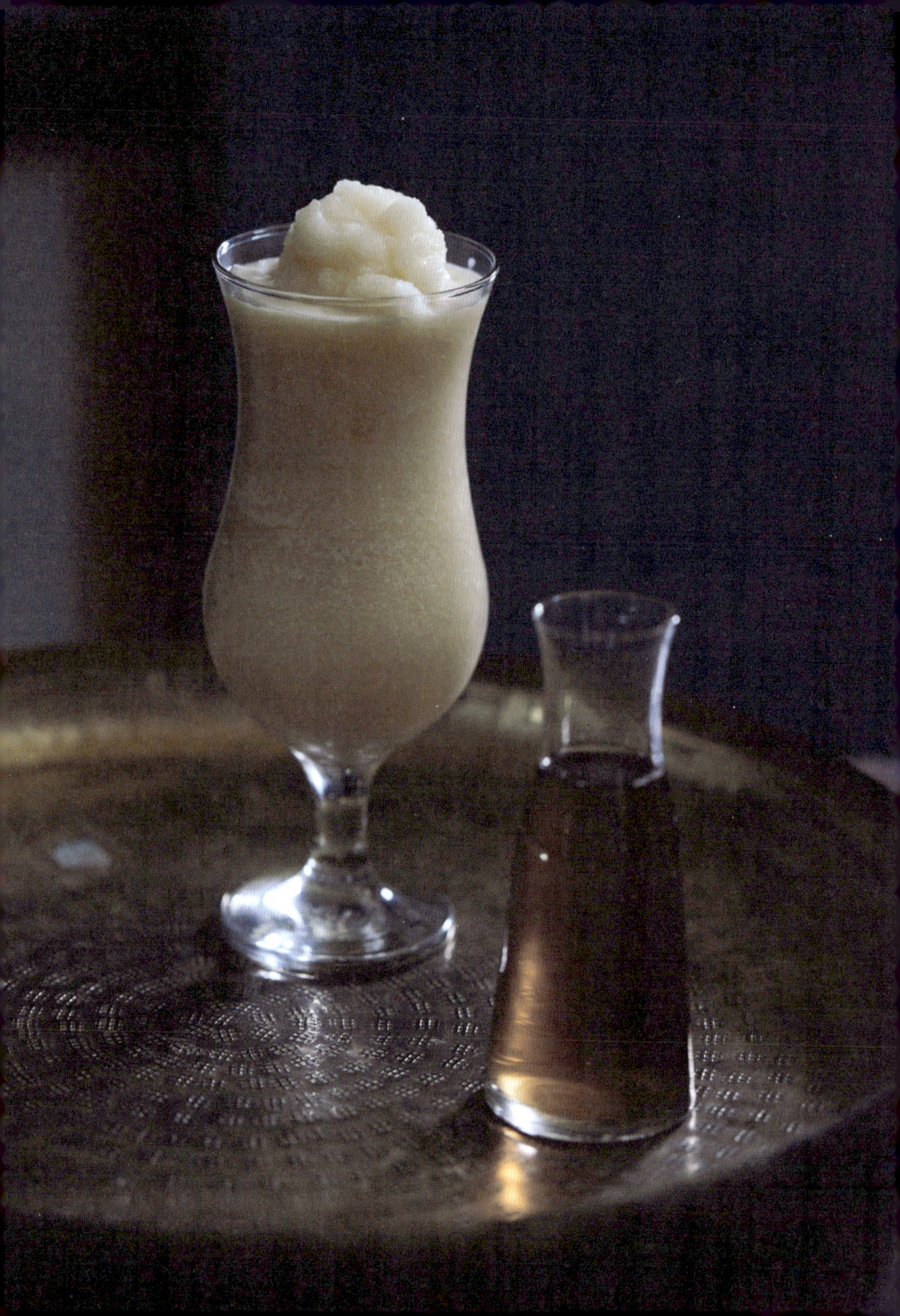

GINGER COLADA

7.3% alc/vol
1.1 standard drinks

23 ml (¾ fl oz) dark rum
15 ml (½ fl oz) ginger brandy
120 ml (4 fl oz) pineapple juice
30 ml (1 fl oz) coconut cream (chilled)

Pour rum, ginger brandy, juice and coconut cream into a blender over a large amount of crushed ice. Blend until slushy and pour into a chilled hurricane glass. Garnish with fresh fruit if desired then serve with a straw.

BANANA COLADA

9.4% alc/vol
1.8 standard drinks

38 ml (1¼ fl oz) light rum
38 ml (1¼ fl oz) banana liqueur
90 ml (3 fl oz) pineapple juice
40 ml (1⅓ fl oz) coconut cream (chilled)
1 teaspoon thick cream (chilled)
1 fresh banana (diced)
maraschino cherry
slice of banana
slice of fresh pineapple

Pour rum, liqueur, juice and creams into a blender over a large amount of crushed ice then add diced banana. Blend until slushy and pour into a chilled hurricane glass. Garnish with a maraschino cherry, slice of banana and a slice of pineapple then serve with a straw.

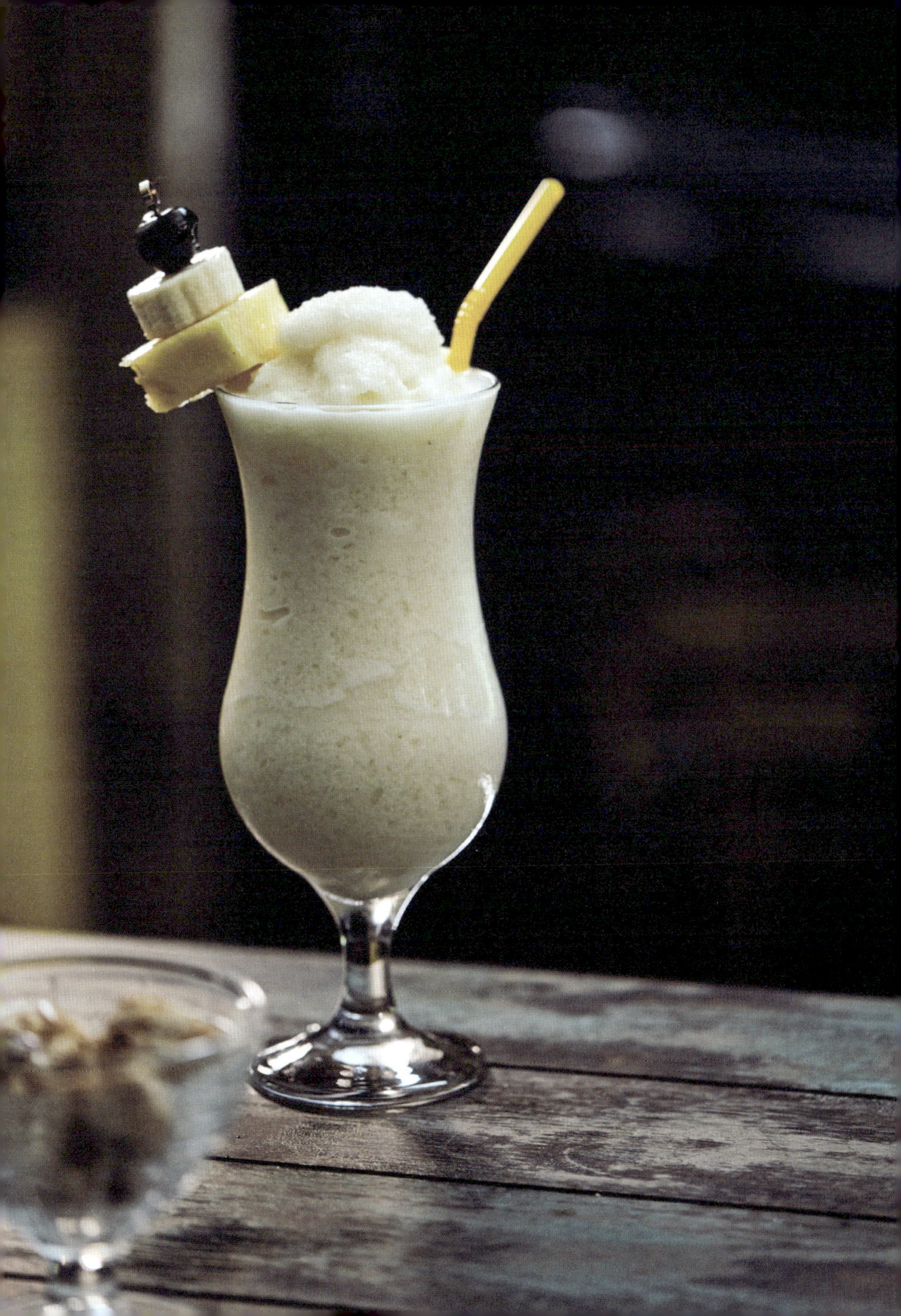

TROPICOLADA

19.1% alc/vol

1.7 standard drinks

38 ml (1¼ fl oz) light rum
15 ml (½ fl oz) banana liqueur
15 ml (½ fl oz) Midori
90 ml (3 fl oz) pineapple juice
40 ml (1⅓ fl oz) coconut cream (chilled)
1 teaspoon thick cream (chilled)

Pour rum, liqueur, Midori, juice and creams into a blender over a large amount of crushed ice then blend until slushy. Pour into a chilled hurricane glass then garnish with fresh fruit if desired. Serve with a straw.

Option: Serve with a slice of fresh pineapple, slice of fresh banana and grated coconut for more tropical flavor.

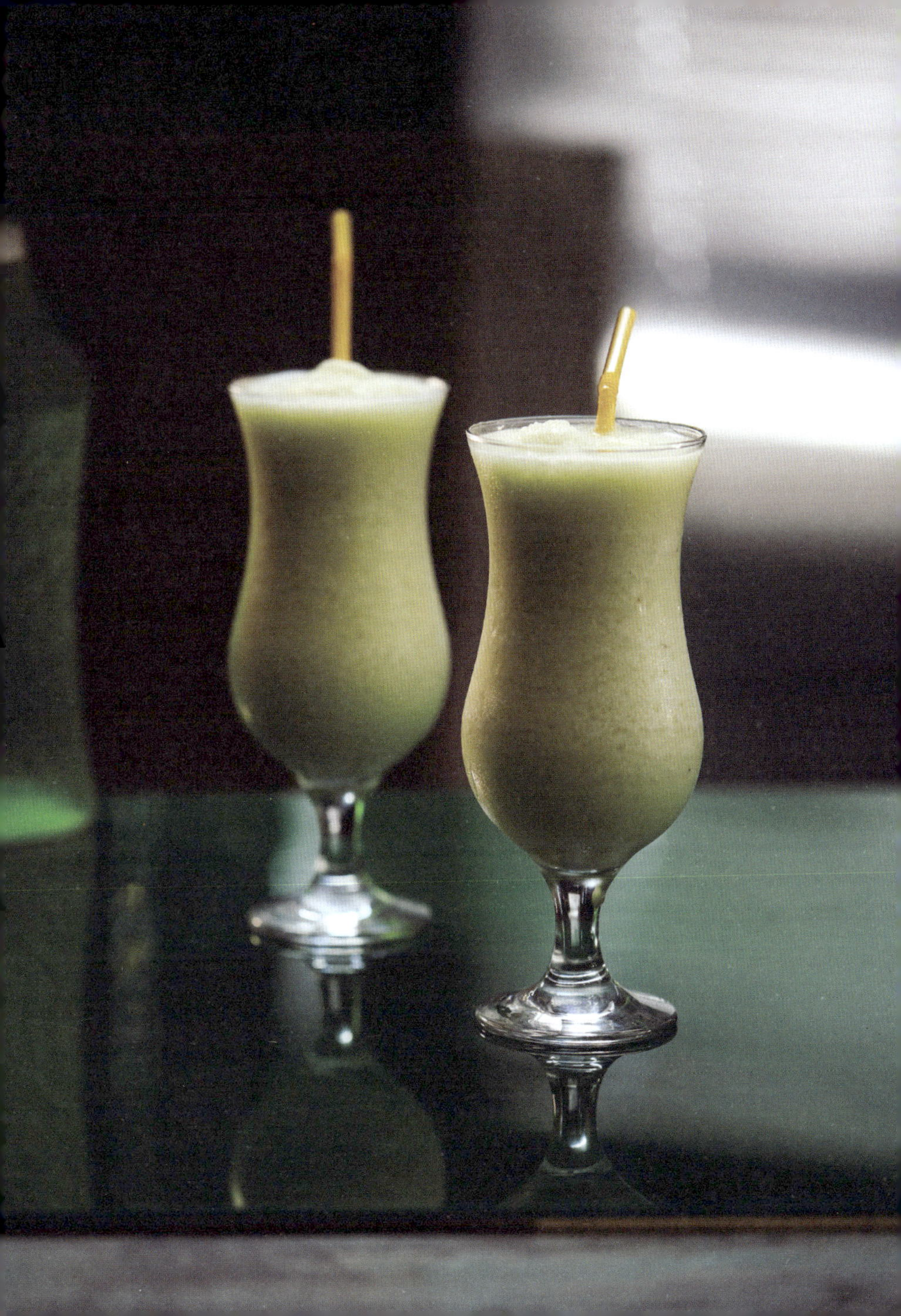

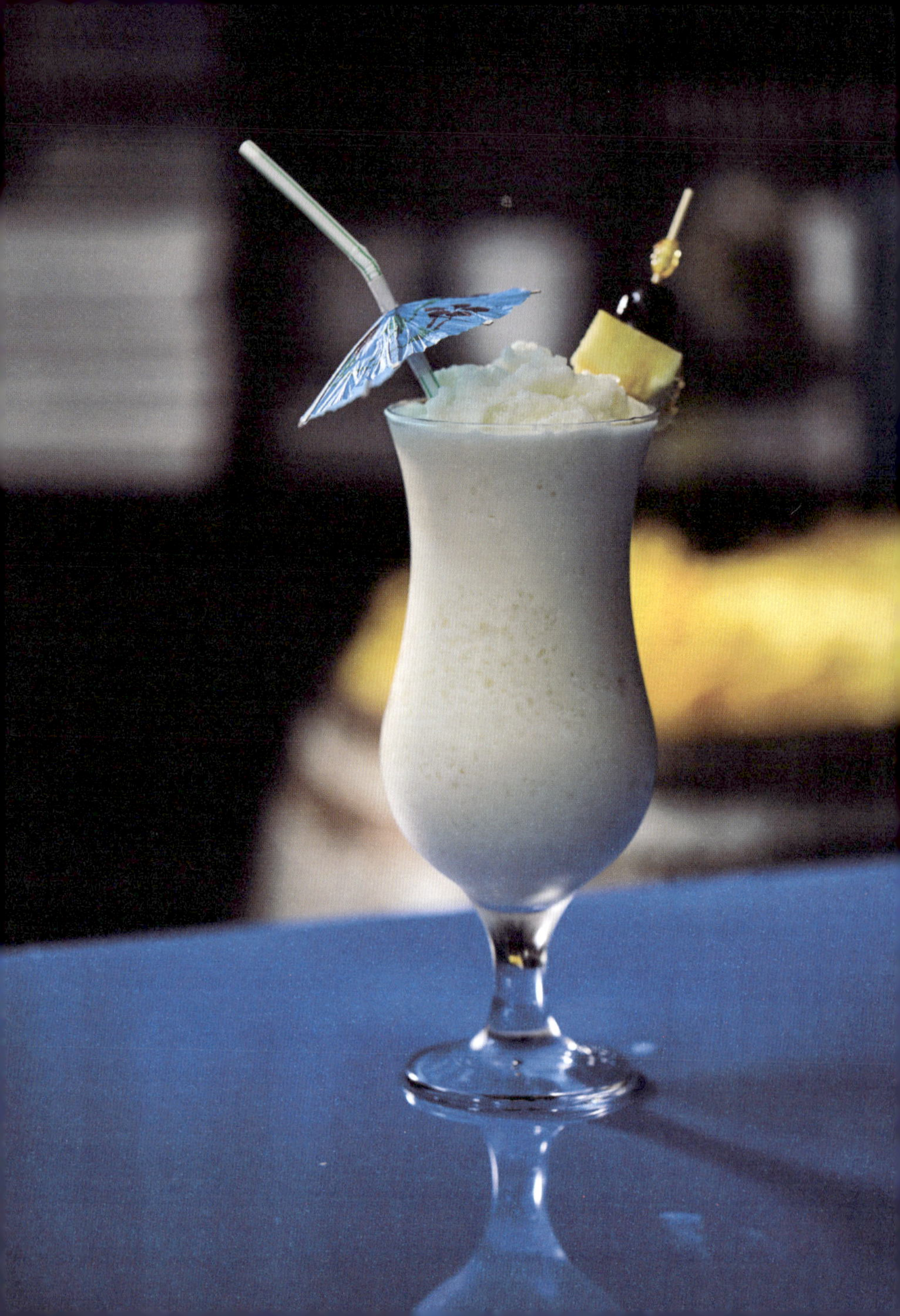

PIÑA COLADA

10.6% alc/vol
1.8 standard drinks

60 ml (2 fl oz) jamaican rum
60 ml (2 fl oz) pineapple juice
60 ml (2 fl oz) thick cream (chilled)
30 ml (1 fl oz) coconut milk (chilled)
maraschino cherry
slice of fresh pineapple

Pour rum, juice, thick cream and coconut milk into a blender over a large amount of crushed ice. Blend until slushy and pour into a chilled hurricane glass. Garnish with a maraschino cherry and a slice of pineapple then serve with a straw.

This drink may also be prepared in a cocktail shaker over a large amount of crushed ice if preferred.

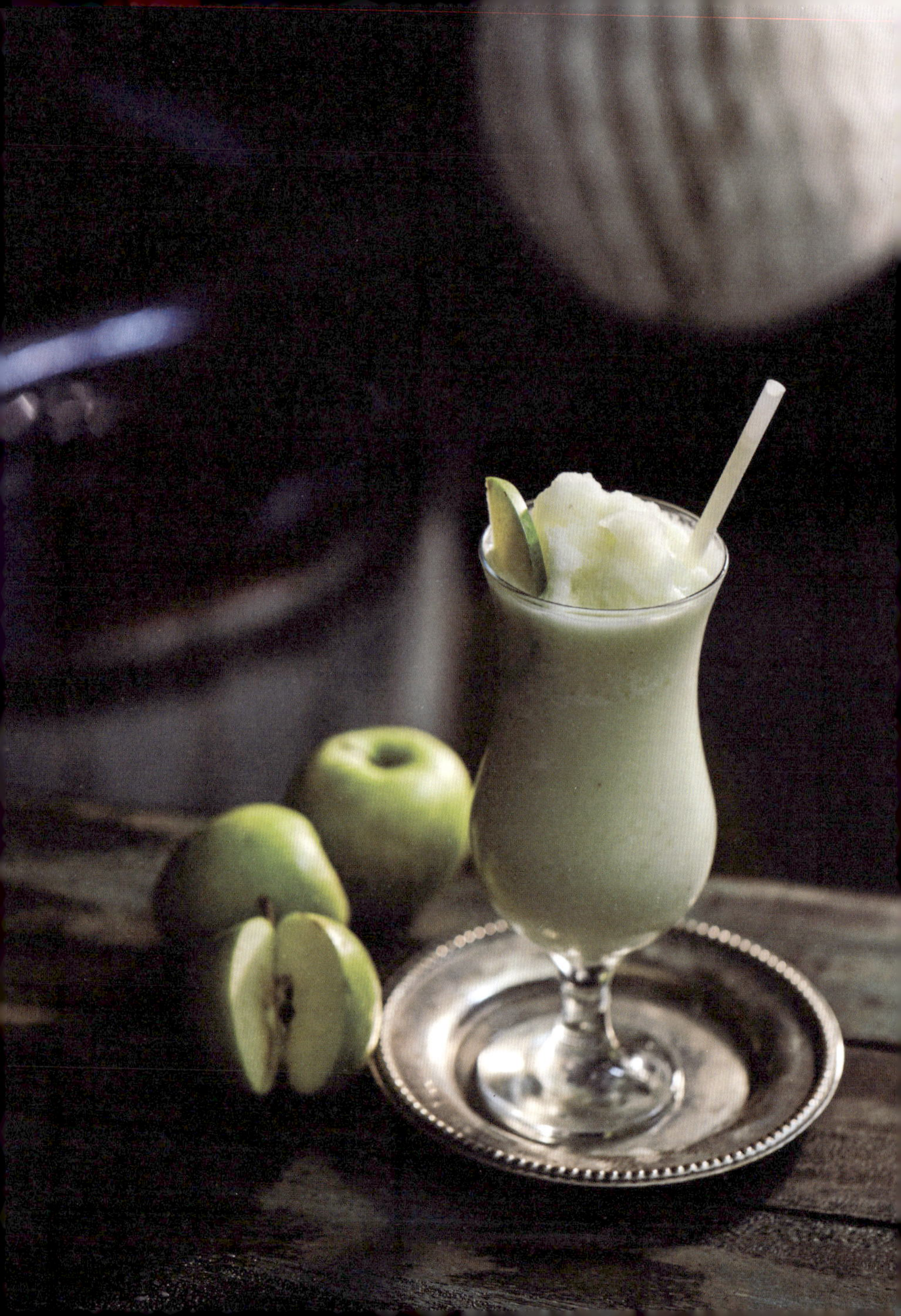

APPLE COLADA

10.3% alc/vol
1.7 standard drinks

38 ml (1¼ fl oz) light rum
38 ml (1¼ fl oz) apple schnapps
90 ml (3 fl oz) pineapple juice
40 ml (1⅓ fl oz) coconut cream (chilled)
1 teaspoon thick cream (chilled)

Pour rum, schnapps, juice and creams into a blender over a large amount of crushed ice then blend until slushy. Pour into a chilled hurricane glass then garnish with fresh fruit of your choice. Serve with a straw.

RASPBERRY COLADA

9.8% alc/vol
1.6 standard drinks

38 ml (1¼ fl oz) light rum
38 ml (1¼ fl oz) Chambord
90 ml (3 fl oz) pineapple juice
40 ml (1⅓ fl oz) coconut cream (chilled)
1 teaspoon thick cream (chilled)
maraschino cherry
slice of fresh pineapple

Pour rum, Chambord, juice and creams into a blender over a large amount of crushed ice. Blend until slushy and pour into a chilled hurricane glass. Garnish with a maraschino cherry and a slice of pineapple then serve with a straw.

PATRIA COLADA

18.3% alc/vol
1.7 standard drinks

30 ml (1 fl oz) light rum
30 ml (1 fl oz) spiced rum
30 ml (1 fl oz) coconut cream (chilled)
30 ml (1 fl oz) passionfruit concentrate
maraschino cherry
pinch of grated coconut

Pour rums and coconut cream into a blender over a large amount of crushed ice then add passionfruit concentrate. Blend until slushy and pour into a chilled hurricane glass then sprinkle grated coconut on top. Garnish with a maraschino cherry then serve with a straw.

COFFEE COLADA

11.6% alc/vol
1.9 standard drinks

38 ml (1¼ fl oz) light rum
38 ml (1¼ fl oz) Tia Maria
90 ml (3 fl oz) pineapple juice
40 ml (1⅓ fl oz) coconut cream (chilled)
1 teaspoon thick cream (chilled)
maraschino cherry
slice of fresh pineapple

Pour rum, Tia Maria, juice and creams into a blender over a large amount of crushed ice. Blend until slushy and pour into a chilled hurricane glass. Garnish with a maraschino cherry and a slice of pineapple then serve a straw.

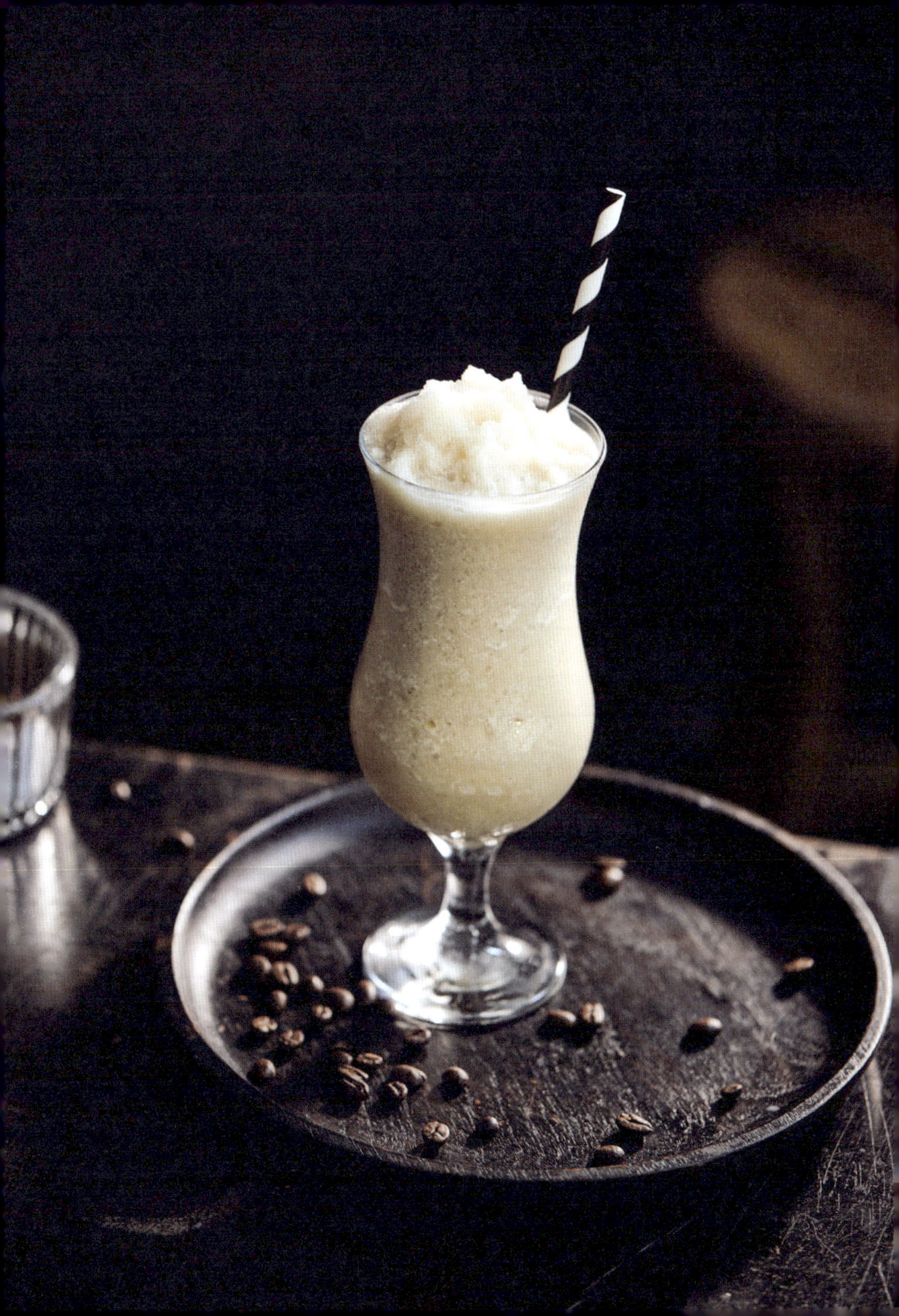

AMARETTO COLADA

11.8% alc/vol
2 standard drinks

38 ml (1¼ fl oz) light rum
38 ml (1¼ fl oz) amaretto
90 ml (3 fl oz) pineapple juice
40 ml (1⅓ fl oz) coconut cream (chilled)
1 teaspoon thick cream (chilled)
maraschino cherry
slice of fresh pineapple

Pour rum, amaretto, juice and creams into a blender over a large amount of crushed ice. Blend until slushy and pour into a chilled hurricane glass. Garnish with a maraschino cherry and a slice of pineapple then serve with a straw.

MELON COLADA

10.5% alc/vol
1.7 standard drinks

38 ml (1¼ fl oz) light rum
38 ml (1¼ fl oz) Midori
90 ml (3 fl oz) pineapple juice
40 ml (1⅓ fl oz) coconut cream (chilled)
1 teaspoon thick cream (chilled)
maraschino cherry
slice of fresh pineapple

Pour rum, Midori, juice and creams into a blender over a large amount of crushed ice. Blend until slushy and pour into a chilled hurricane glass. Garnish with a maraschino cherry and a slice of pineapple then serve with a straw.

COCOA COLADA

17.4% alc/vol

1.8 standard drinks

45 ml (1½ fl oz) light rum
15 ml (½ fl oz) coconut liqueur
8 ml (¼ fl oz) Kahlúa
45 ml (1½ fl oz) fresh milk (chilled)
15 ml (½ fl oz) chocolate syrup
pinch of grated chocolate

Pour rum, liqueur, Kahlúa, milk and chocolate syrup into a blender over a large amount of crushed ice then blend until slushy. Pour into a chilled hurricane glass and sprinkle grated chocolate on top. Serve with a straw.

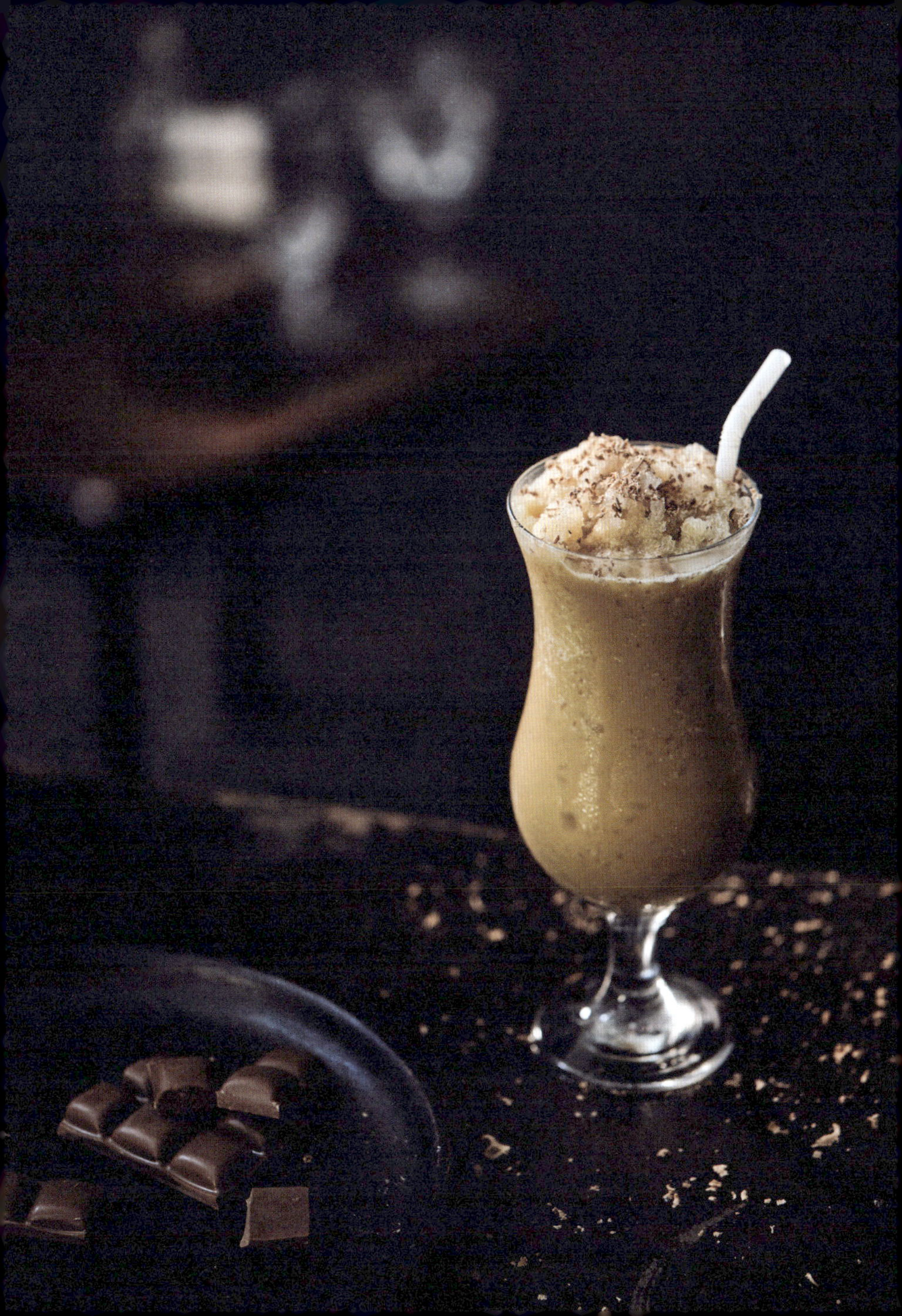

BLUE COLADA

10.8% alc/vol
1.7 standard drinks

38 ml (1¼ fl oz) light rum
30 ml (1 fl oz) blue Curaçao
90 ml (3 fl oz) pineapple juice
40 ml (1⅓ fl oz) coconut cream (chilled)
1 teaspoon thick cream (chilled)

Pour rum, Curaçao, juice and creams into a blender over a large amount of crushed ice. Blend until slushy and pour into a chilled hurricane glass. Garnish with fresh fruit of your choice and a blue straw.

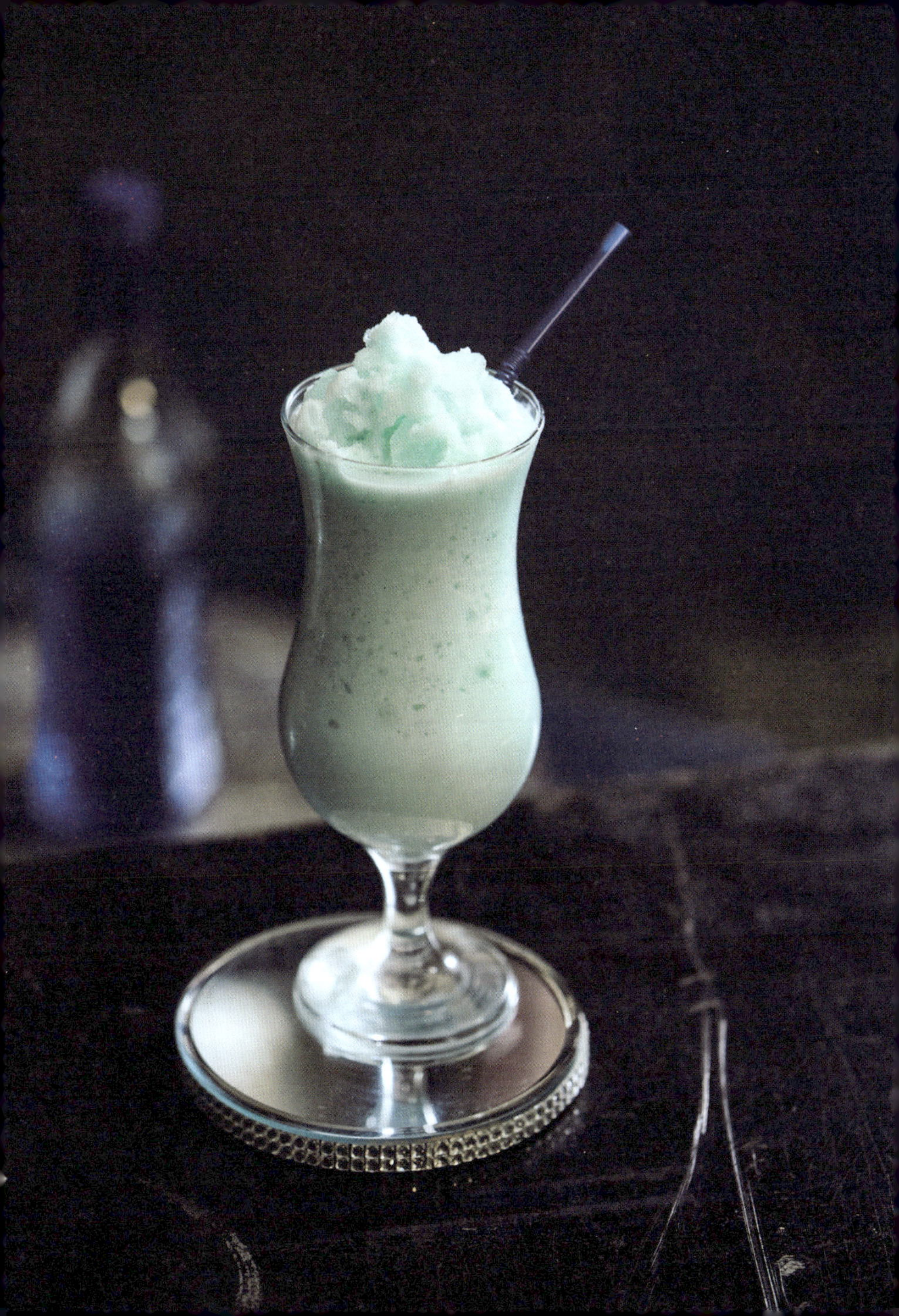

ST. MARTIN COLADA

12.8% alc/vol
1.6 standard drinks

38 ml (1¼ fl oz) spiced rum
30 ml (1 fl oz) coconut liqueur
90 ml (3 fl oz) pineapple juice
slice of fresh pineapple

Pour rum, liqueur and juice into a blender over a large amount of crushed ice then blend until slushy. Pour into a chilled hurricane glass and garnish with a slice of pineapple then serve with a straw.

COLADA COLLISION

4.5% alc/vol
1.3 standard drinks

45 ml (1½ fl oz) light rum
180 ml (6 fl oz) pineapple juice
90 ml (3 fl oz) coconut cream (chilled)
1 fresh banana (diced)
slice of fresh banana
slice of fresh pineapple

Pour rum, juice and coconut cream into a blender over a large amount of crushed ice then add diced banana. Blend until slushy and pour into a chilled hurricane glass. Garnish with slices of banana and pineapple then serve with a straw.

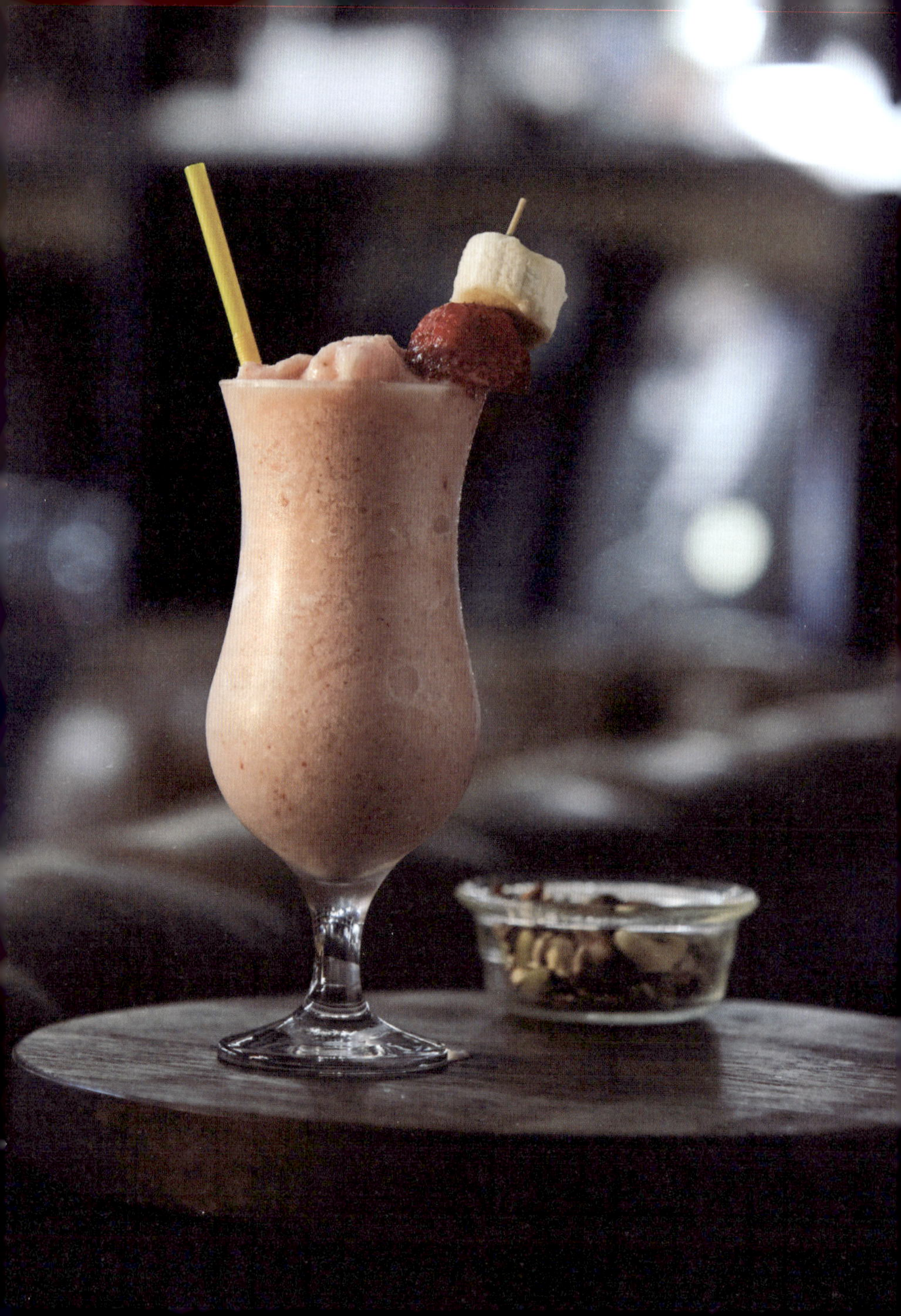

STRAWBERRY BANANA COLADA

6.4% alc/vol
1.1 standard drinks

38 ml (1¼ fl oz) light rum
60 ml (2 fl oz) coconut cream (chilled)
6 fresh strawberries (diced)
1 fresh banana (diced)
slice of fresh banana
fresh strawberry

Pour rum and coconut cream into a blender over a large amount of crushed ice. Add diced strawberries and diced banana then blend until slushy. Pour into a chilled hurricane glass then garnish with slices of banana and strawberry. Serve with a straw.

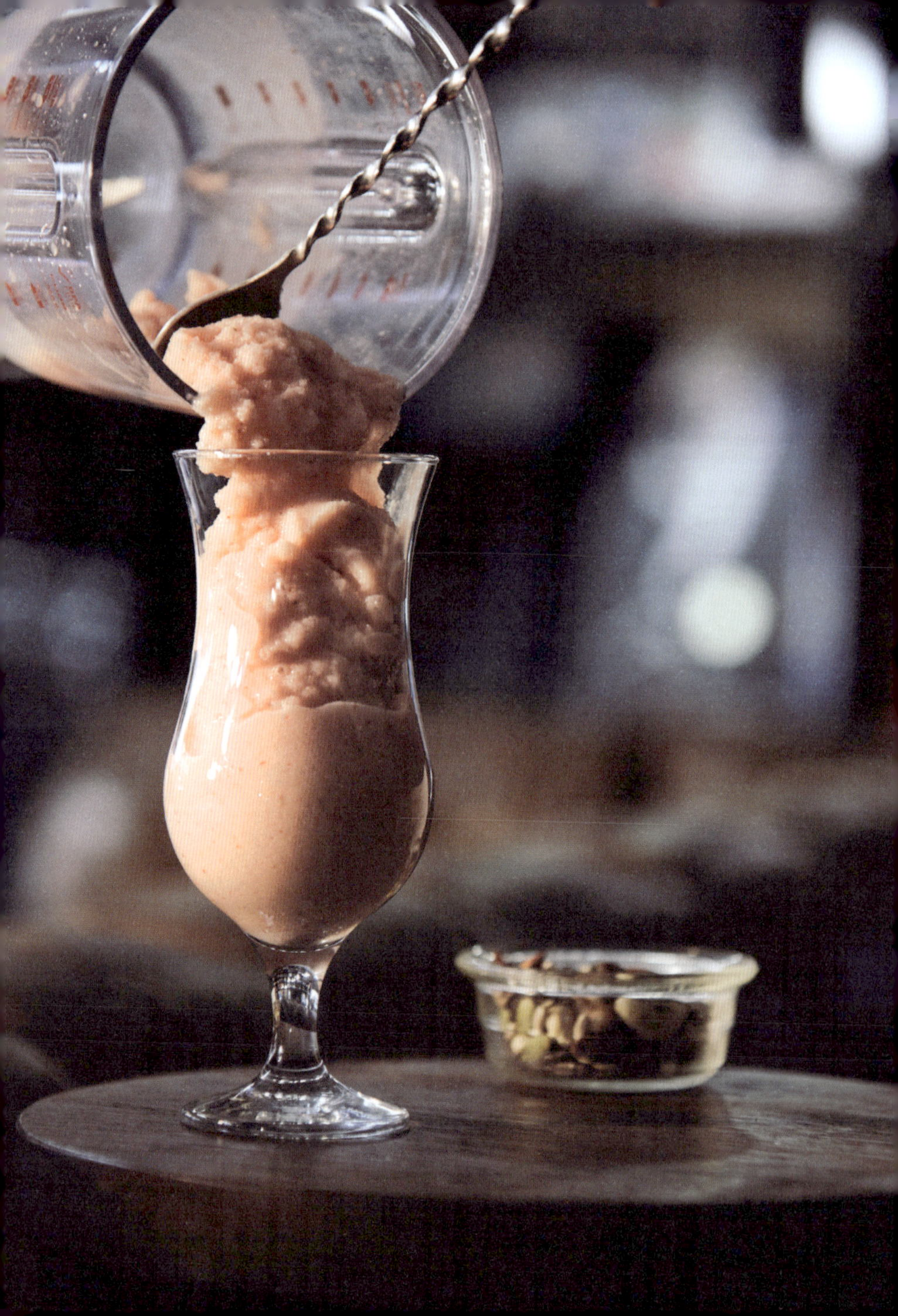

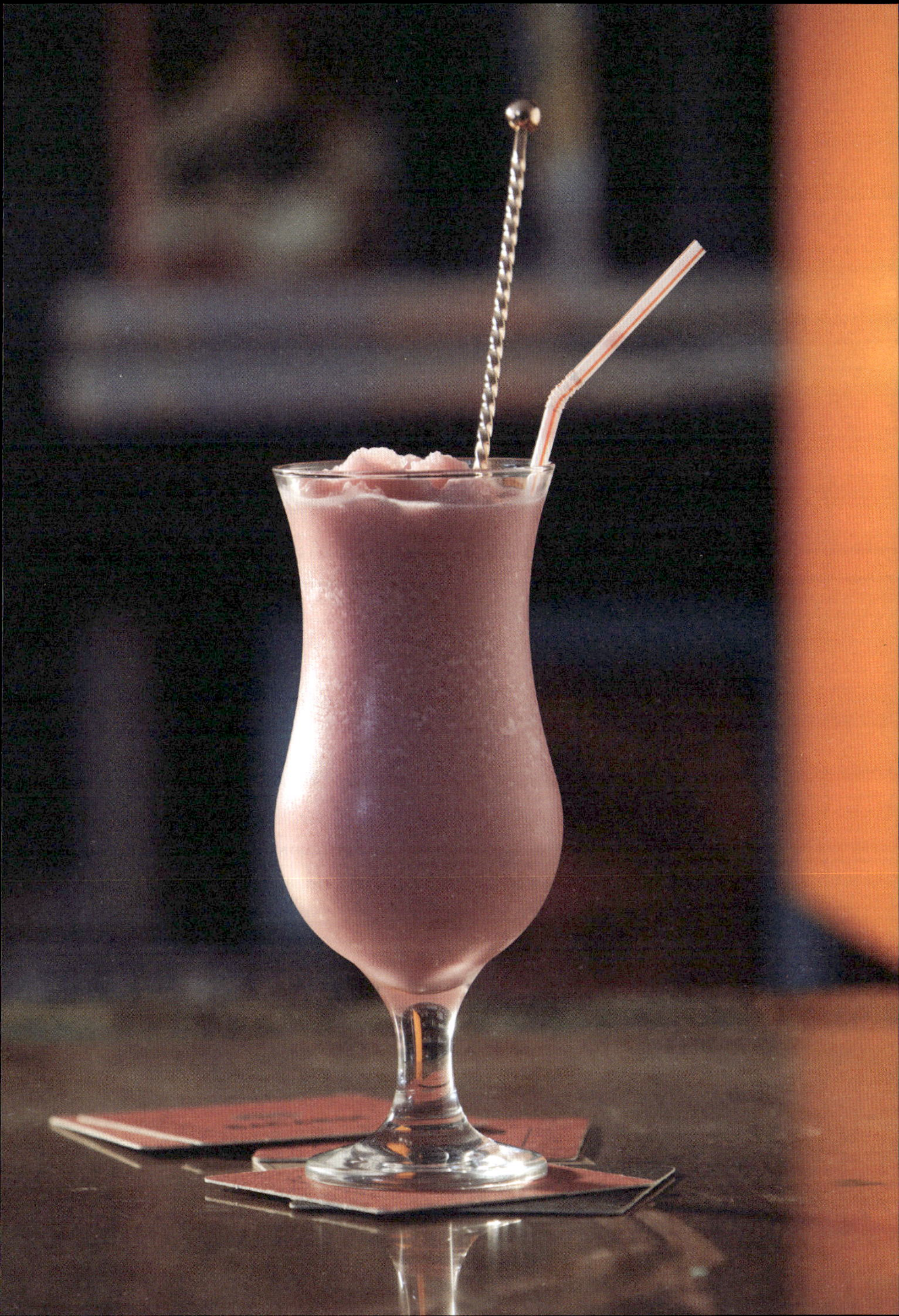

CHAMBORLADA

14.5% alc/vol

3.4 standard drinks

60 ml (2 fl oz) Bacardi
60 ml (2 fl oz) Chambord
30 ml (1 fl oz) dark rum
90 ml (3 fl oz) pineapple juice
60 ml (2 fl oz) coconut cream (chilled)

Pour 30 ml (1 fl oz) Chambord into a chilled hurricane glass then pour Bacardi, rum, juice and coconut cream into a blender over a large amount of crushed ice. Blend until slushy and pour gently into the glass over Chambord – do not stir. Layer remaining 30 ml (1 fl oz) Chambord on top then serve with a swizzle stick and a straw.

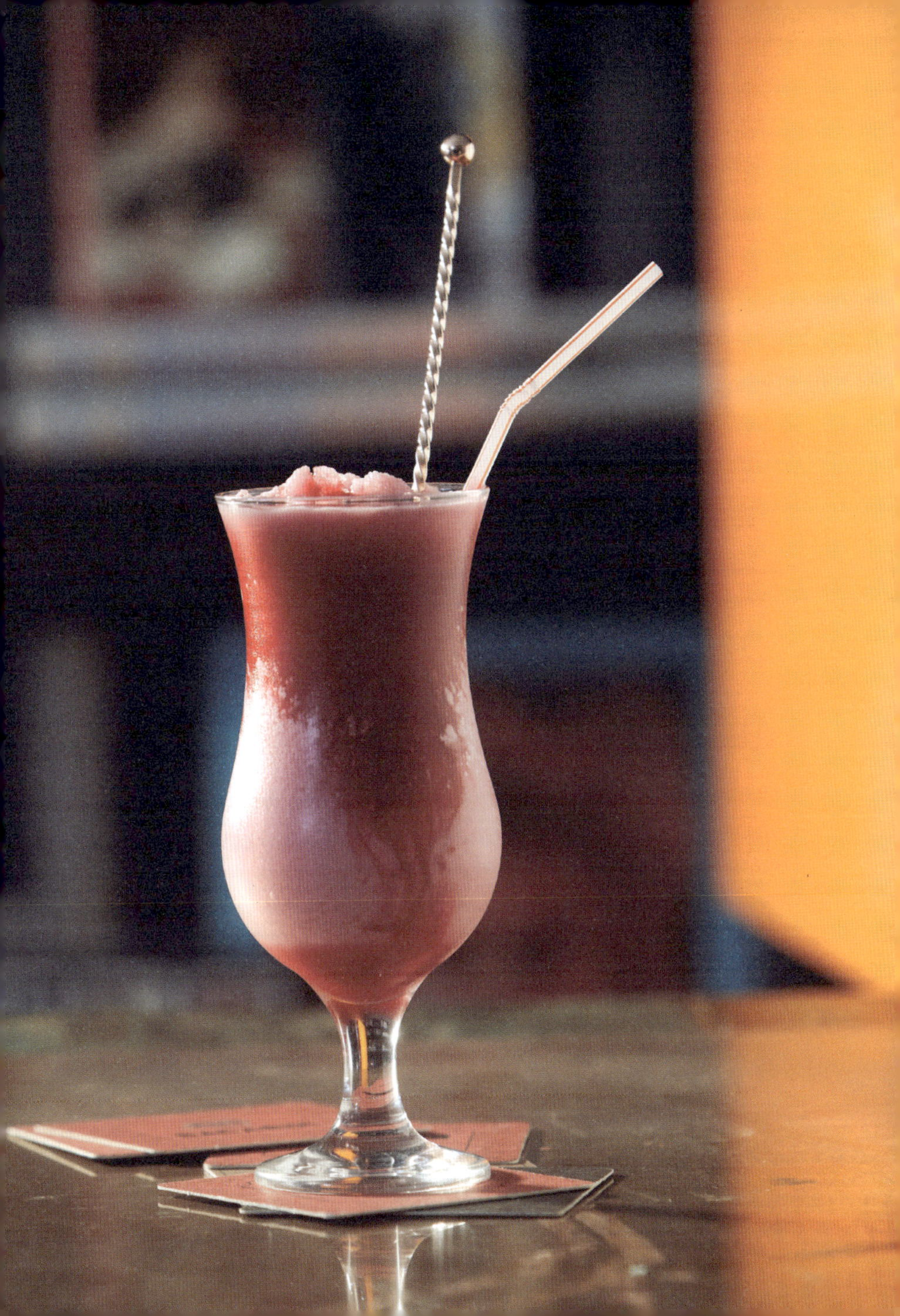

♦ ♦ ♦

The daiquiri is a Bacardi-based cocktail that originated from Cuba around 1905. It is believed to have been created by Jennings Cox who was an American working in the town of Daiquiri at an iron mine. Daiquiris became very popular in America during the 1940's, so much so that the 19th July each year is celebrated as National Daiquiri Day.

Today there are many varieties of the daiquiri cocktail with the majority being served in champagne saucers or cocktail glasses.

♦ ♦ ♦

Daiquiri
COCKTAILS

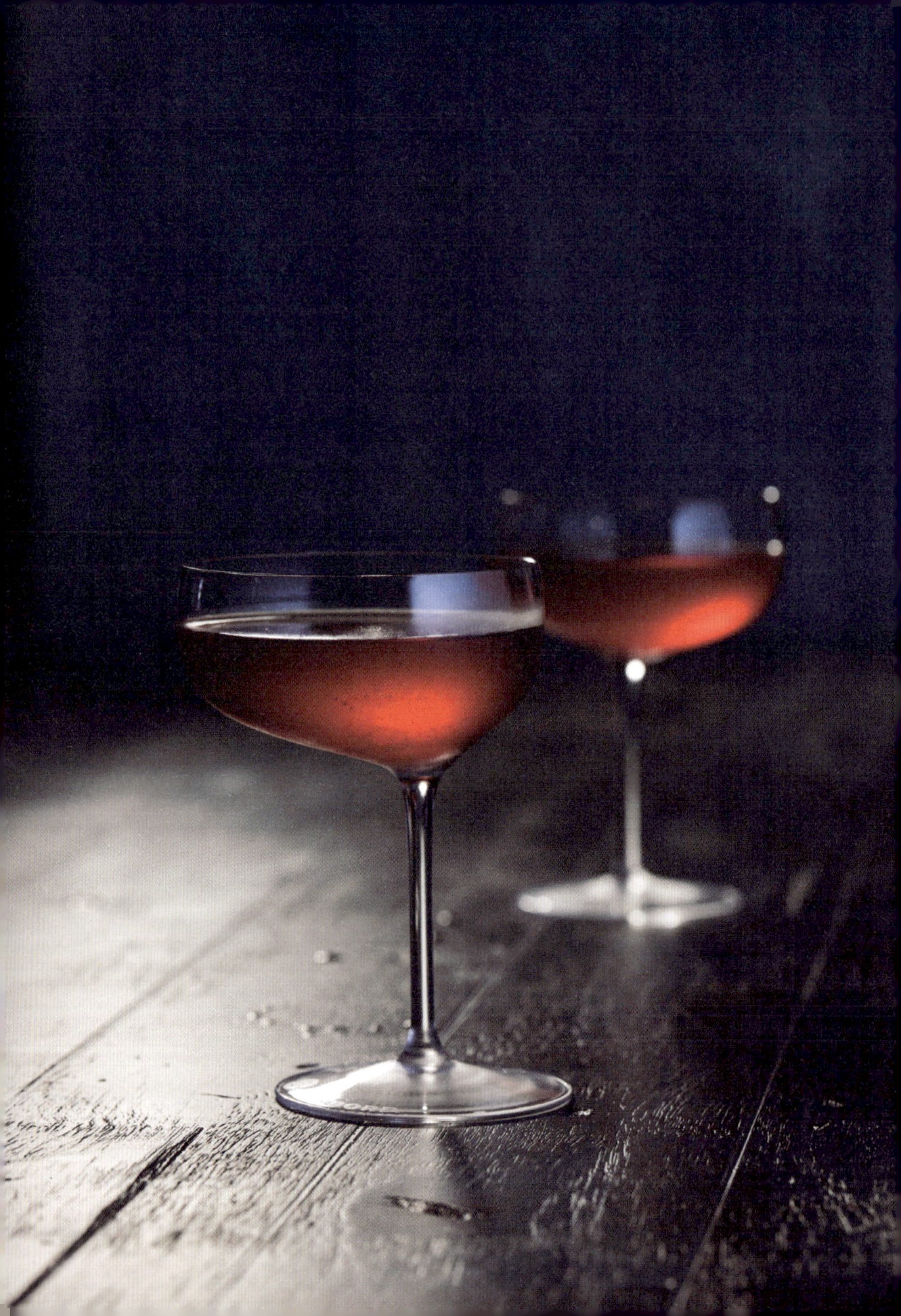

CLASSIC DAIQUIRI

25.6% alc/vol

1.4 standard drinks

45 ml (1½ fl oz) Bacardi
5 ml (⅙ fl oz) grenadine
15 ml (½ fl oz) fresh lime juice

Pour ingredients into a cocktail shaker over ice and shake. Strain into a chilled cocktail glass and serve.

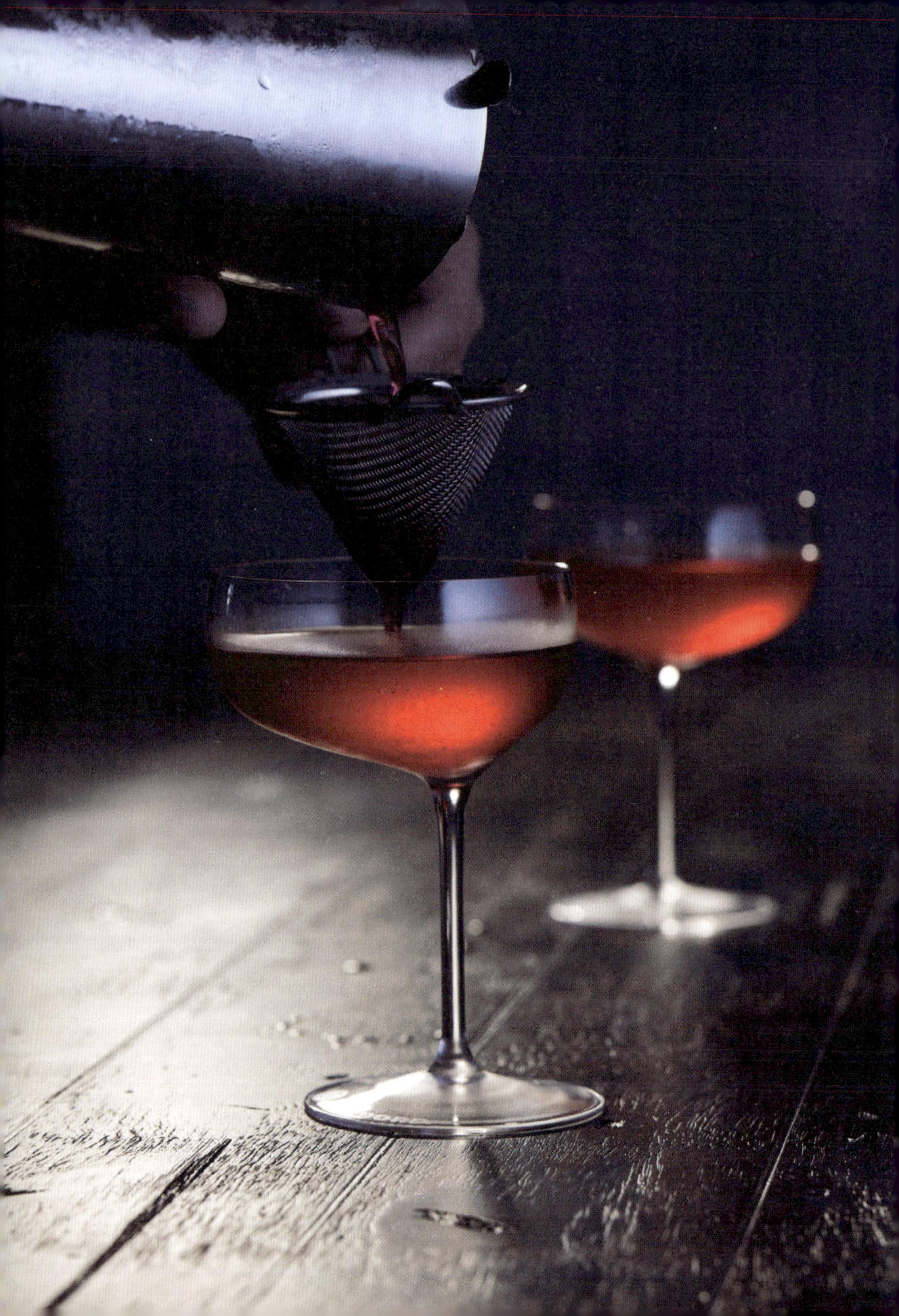

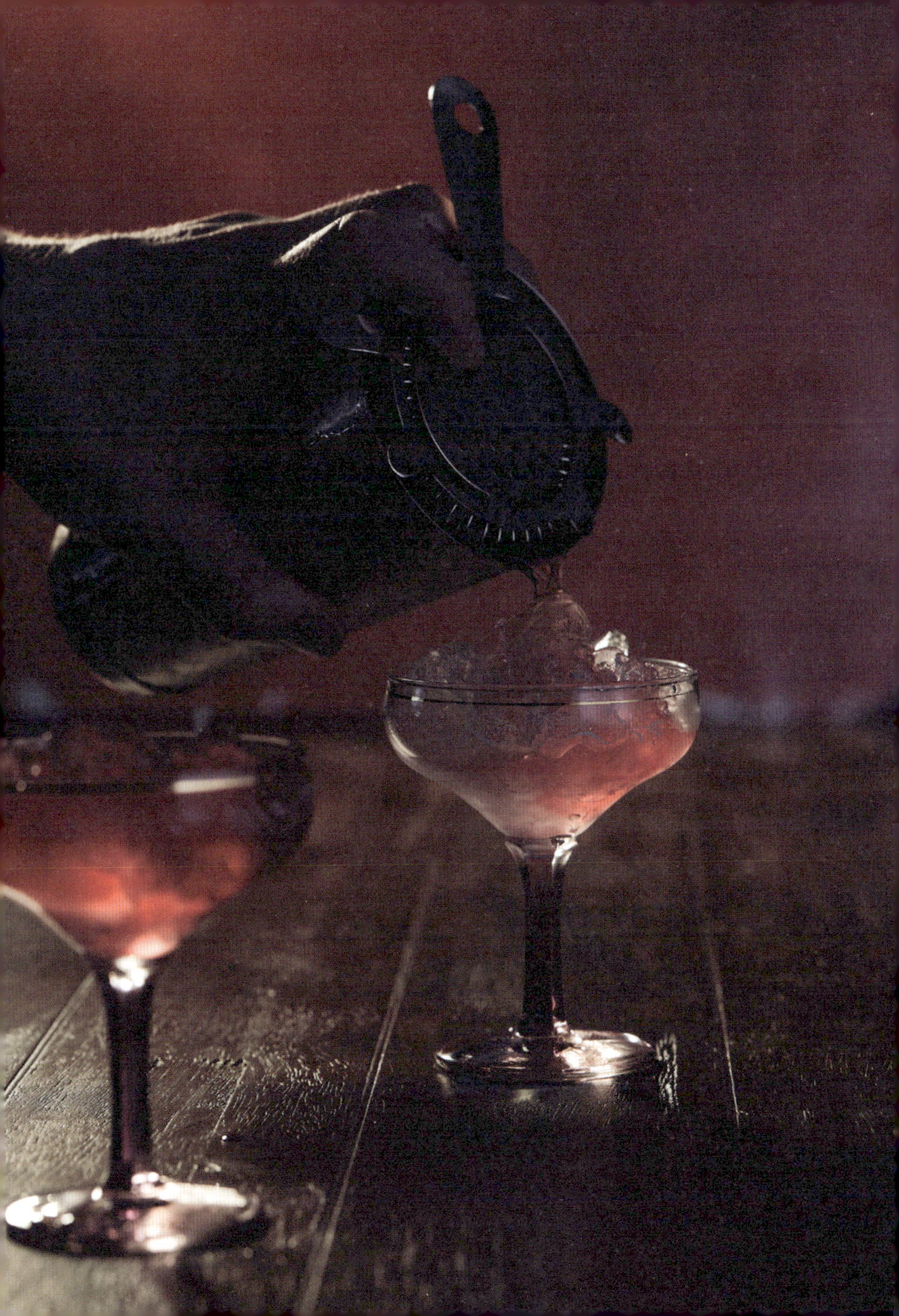

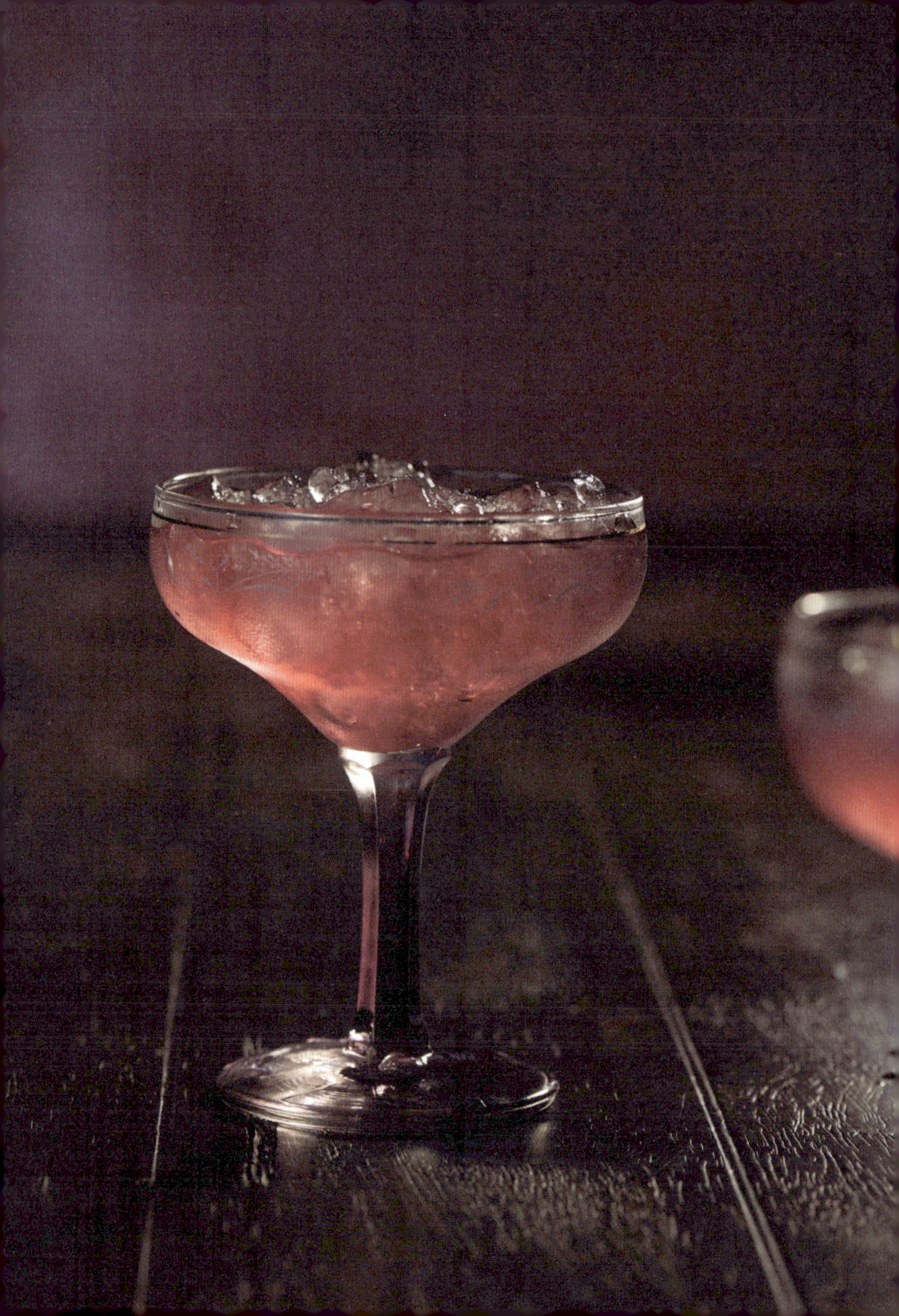

FROZEN DAIQUIRI

26.3% alc/vol
1.4 standard drinks

This drink is a Daiquiri that is served in a cocktail glass half-filled with crushed ice – page 11.

A dash of maraschino liqueur may also be added if desired.

GALLIANO DAIQUIRI

26.3% alc/vol
1.5 standard drinks

30 ml (1 fl oz) Bacardi
20 ml (⅔ fl oz) Galliano
15 ml (½ fl oz) fresh lime juice
1 teaspoon sugar syrup

Pour ingredients into a cocktail shaker over ice and shake. Strain into a chilled cocktail glass and serve with a short yellow straw.

THE ALL-AMERICAN DAIQUIRI

9.9% alc/vol
1.4 standard drinks

Step 1:
23 ml (¾ fl oz) Bacardi
45 ml (1½ fl oz) sweet & sour mix
15 ml (½ fl oz) blueberry syrup

Step 2:
23 ml (¾ fl oz) Bacardi
60 ml (2 fl oz) strawberry daiquiri mix

Step 3:
fresh whipped cream (chilled)
maraschino cherry

Blend steps 1 and 2 in separate blenders over a large amount of crushed ice until each is slushy and evenly blended. Pour step 1 into a chilled margarita glass then pour step 2 into the glass to layer on top of step 1 and float whipped cream on top. Garnish with a maraschino cherry then serve with a short blue straw and a short red straw.

BACARDI DAIQUIRI

24.4% alc/vol

1.3 standard drinks

45 ml (1½ fl oz) Bacardi
5 ml (⅙ fl oz) grenadine
15 ml (½ fl oz) fresh lemon or lime juice
1 teaspoon egg white
maraschino cherry

Pour Bacardi, grenadine, lemon or lime juice as desired and egg white into a cocktail shaker over ice then shake well. Strain into a chilled cocktail glass and garnish with a maraschino cherry then serve.

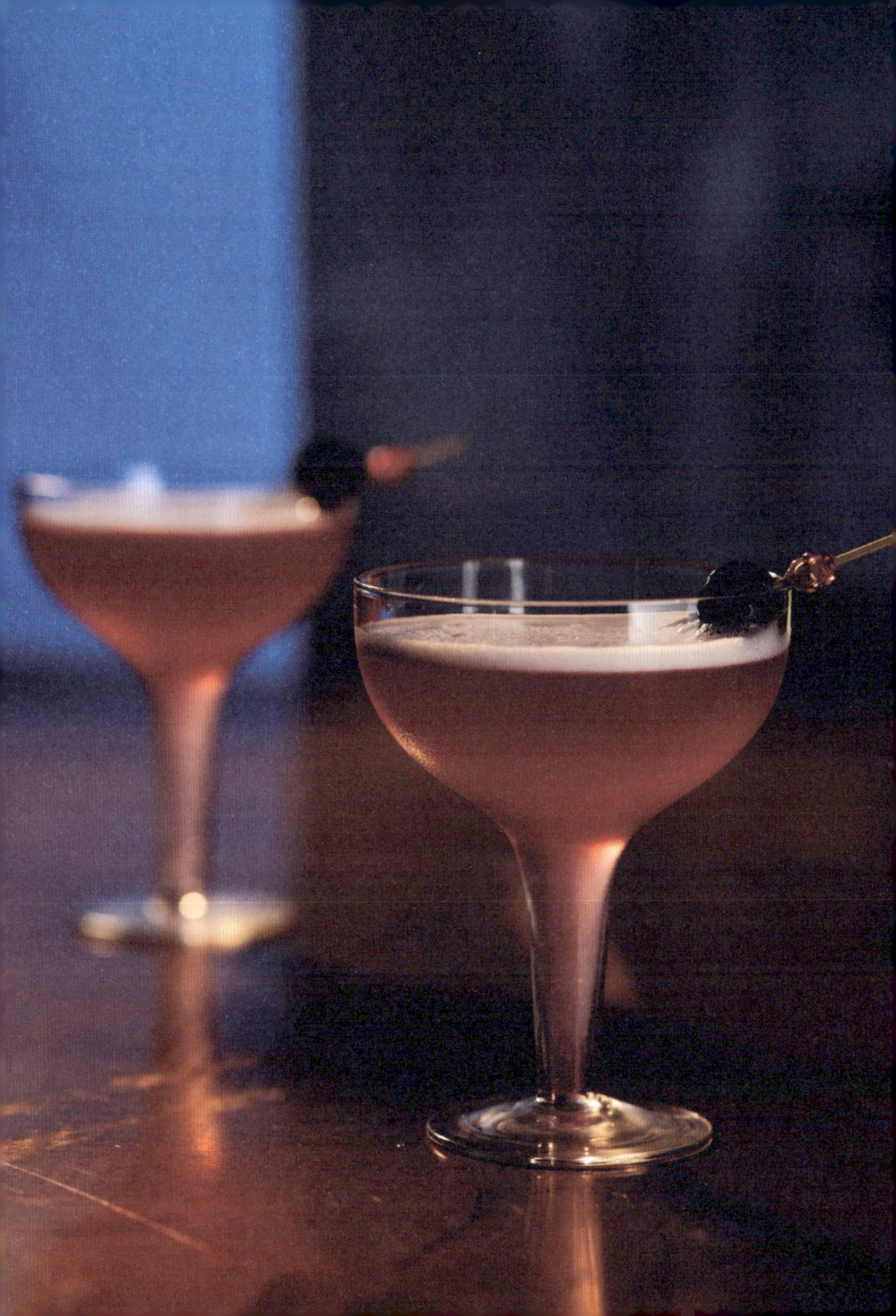

STRAWBERRY DAIQUIRI

16% alc/vol

1.6 standard drinks

30 ml (1 fl oz) Bacardi
15 ml (½ fl oz) Cointreau
15 ml (½ fl oz) strawberry liqueur
30 ml (1 fl oz) fresh lemon juice
4 fresh strawberries (diced)
fresh strawberry

Pour Bacardi, Cointreau, liqueur and juice into a blender over small amount of crushed ice then add diced strawberries. Blend until smooth and pour into a chilled cocktail glass. Garnish with a strawberry and serve.

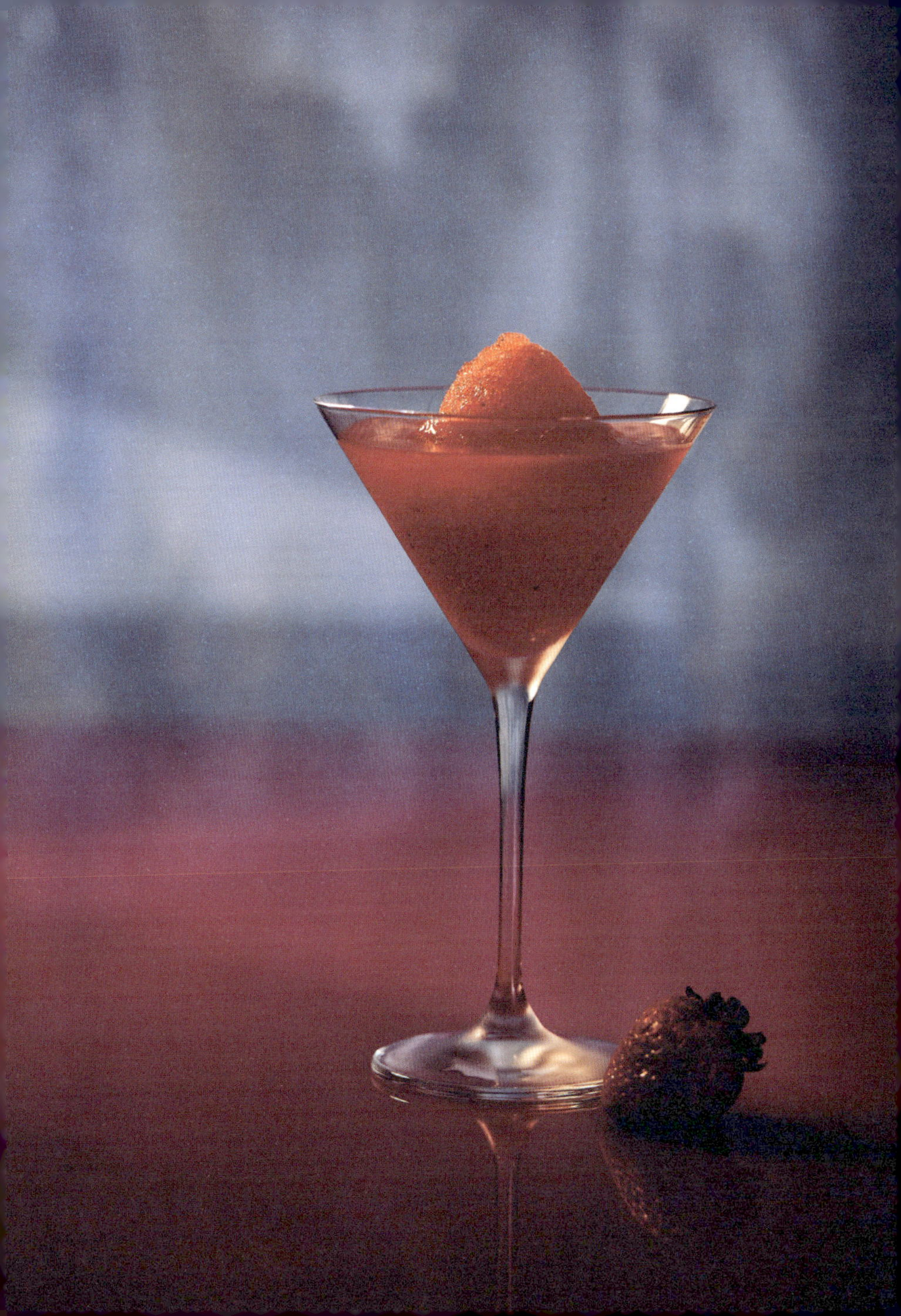

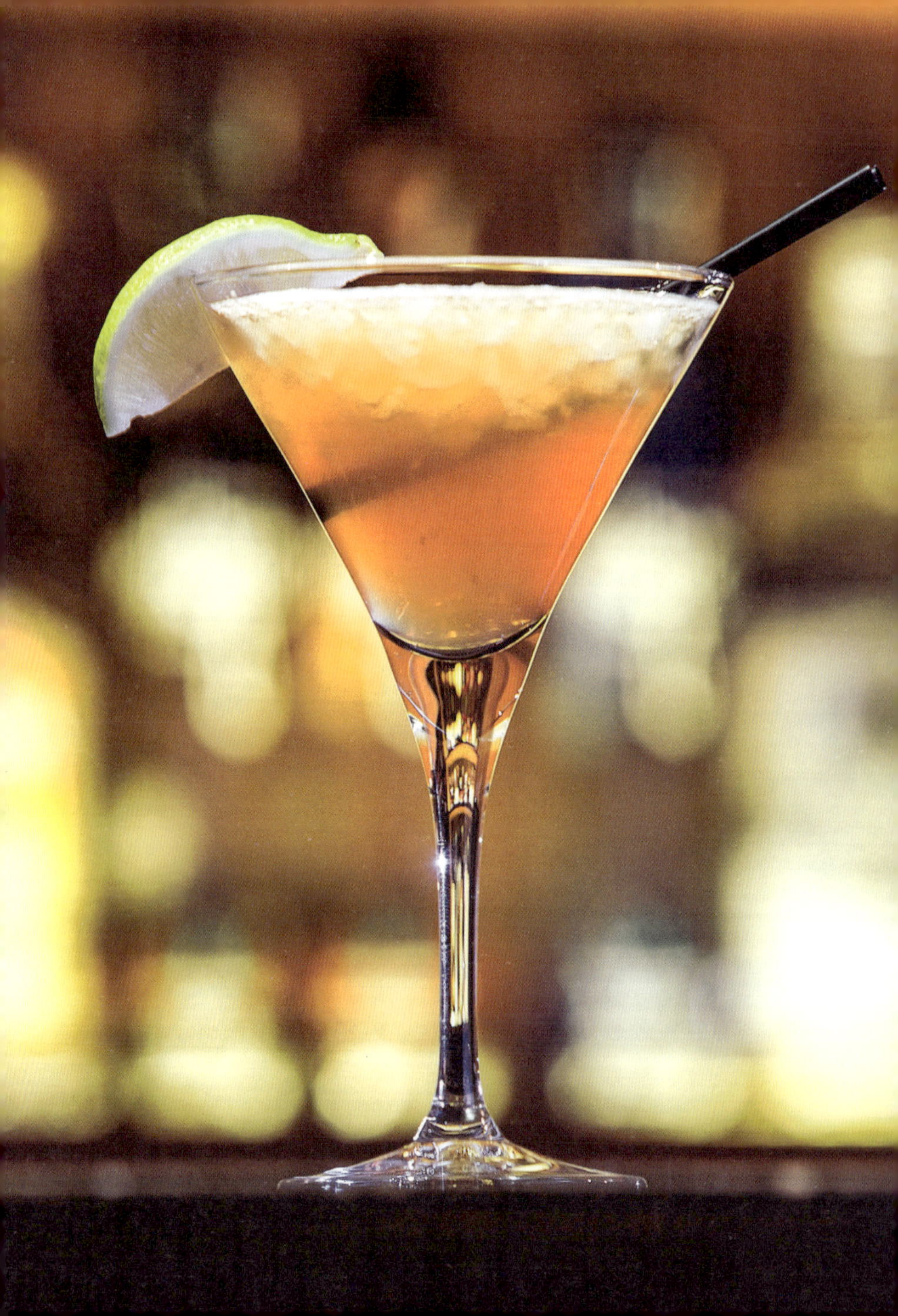

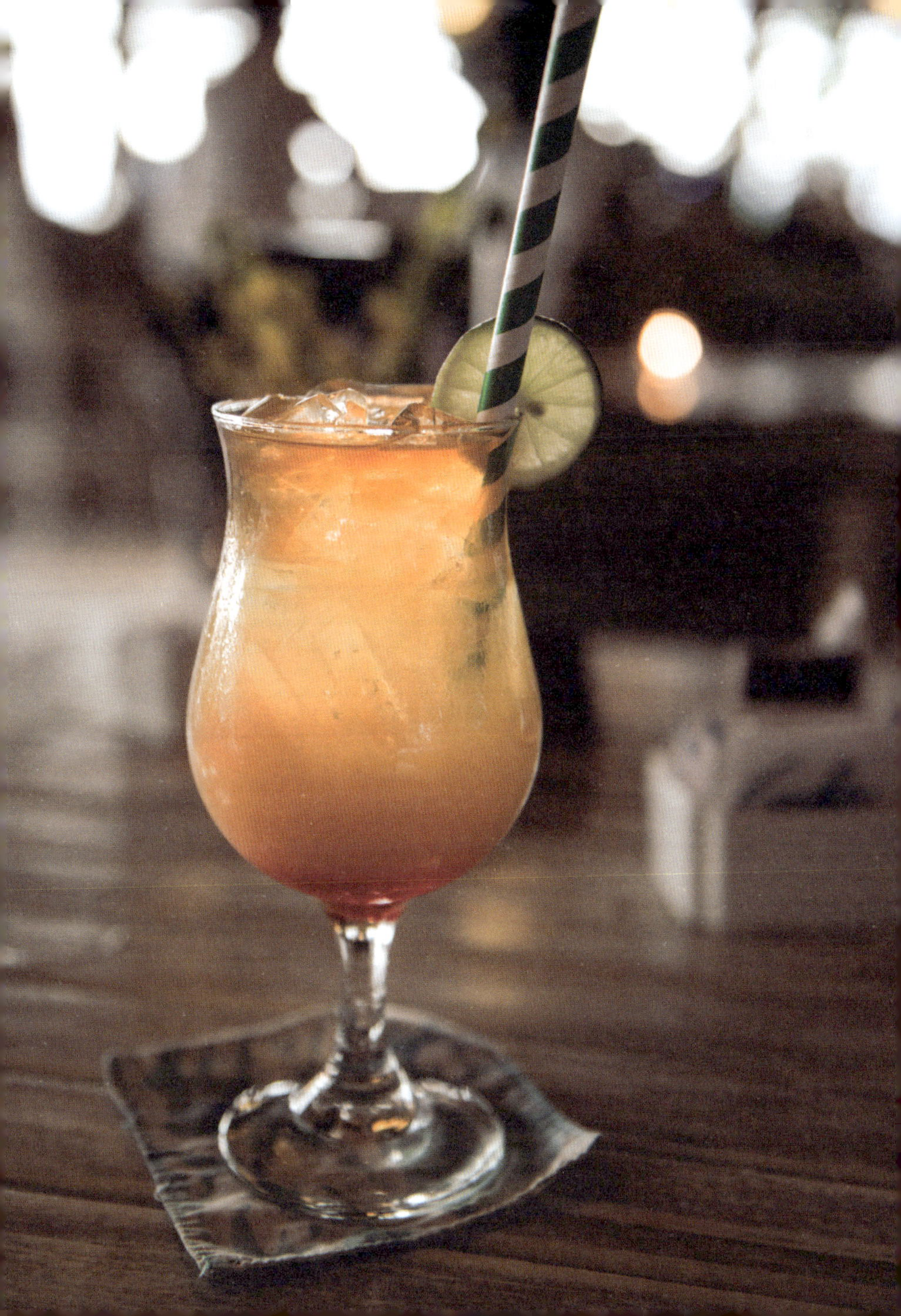

MANGO DAIQUIRI

11.5% alc/vol
1.6 standard drinks

30 ml (1 fl oz) Bacardi
15 ml (½ fl oz) Cointreau
15 ml (½ fl oz) mango liqueur
30 ml (1 fl oz) fresh lemon juice
1 fresh mango (diced)
slice of fresh mango

Pour Bacardi, Cointreau, liqueur and juice into a blender over a small amount of crushed ice then add diced mango. Blend until smooth and pour into a chilled cocktail glass. Garnish with a slice of mango and serve with a straw.

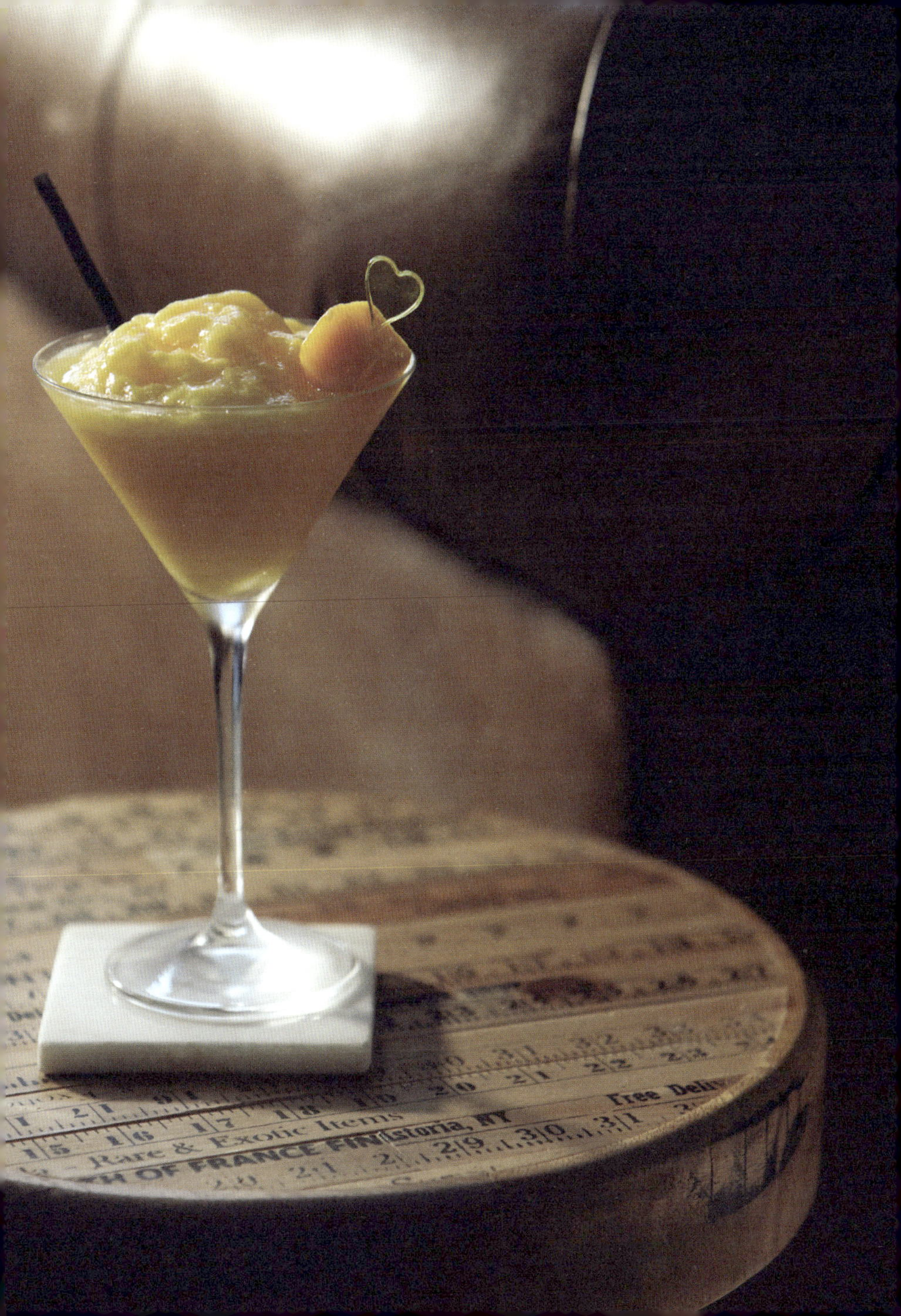
Rare & Exotic Items
Astoria, NY

FROZEN BLUE DAIQUIRI

29.2% alc/vol

2.1 standard drinks

60 ml (2 fl oz) Bacardi
15 ml (½ fl oz) blue Curaçao
15 ml (½ fl oz) fresh lime juice

Pour ingredients into a blender over a large amount of crushed ice and blend until slushy. Pour into a frosted cocktail glass and serve with a short blue straw.

CHERRY DAIQUIRI

26.8% alc/vol
2.3 standard drinks

45 ml (1½ fl oz) Bacardi
30 ml (1 fl oz) cherry brandy
15 ml (½ fl oz) kirsch
15 ml (½ fl oz) fresh lime juice
1 teaspoon sugar syrup
maraschino cherry
twist of fresh lemon peel

Pour Bacardi, cherry brandy, kirsch, juice and sugar into a cocktail shaker over ice. Shake well and strain into a chilled cocktail glass. Garnish with a maraschino cherry and twist of lemon peel then serve with a short red straw.

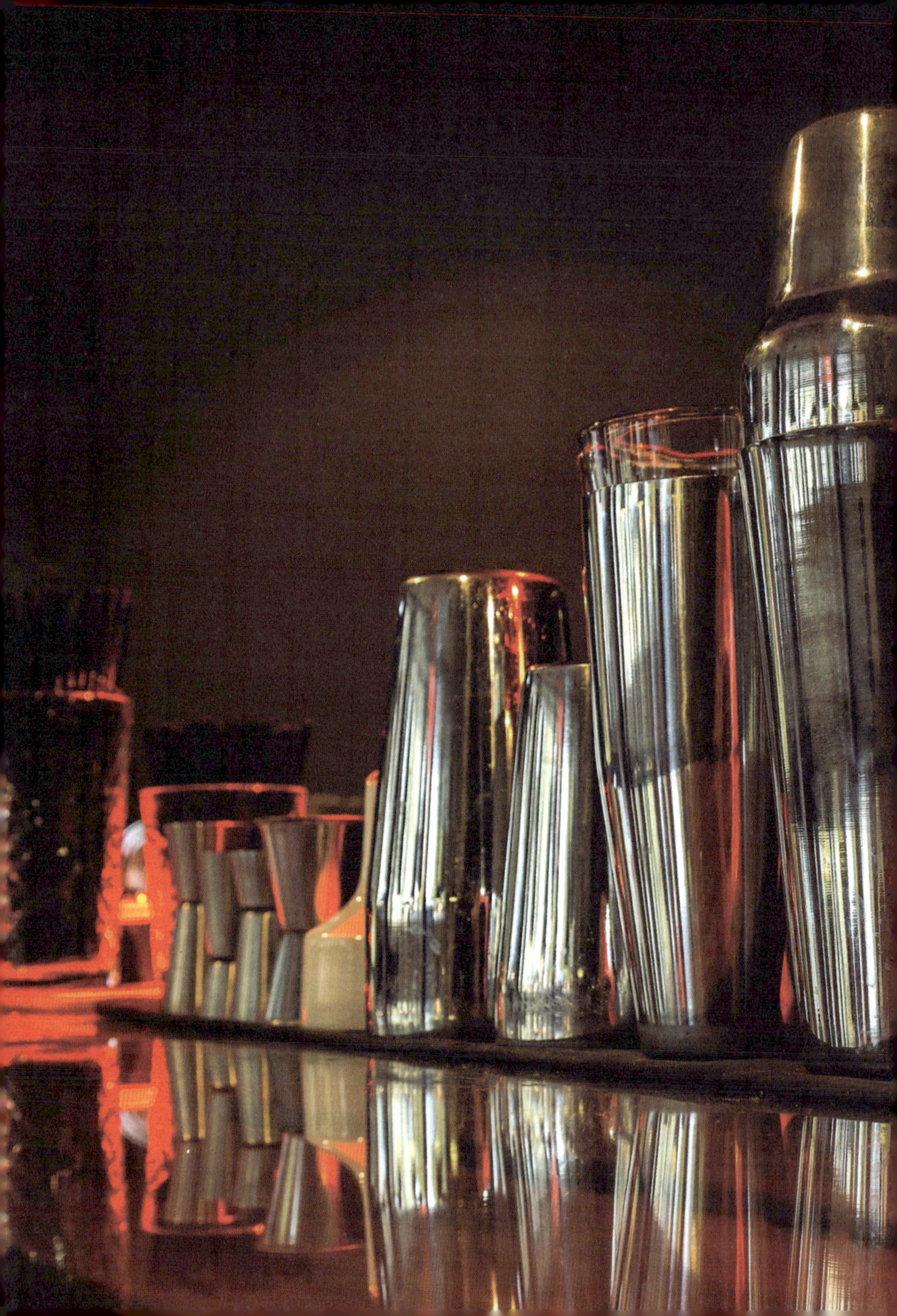

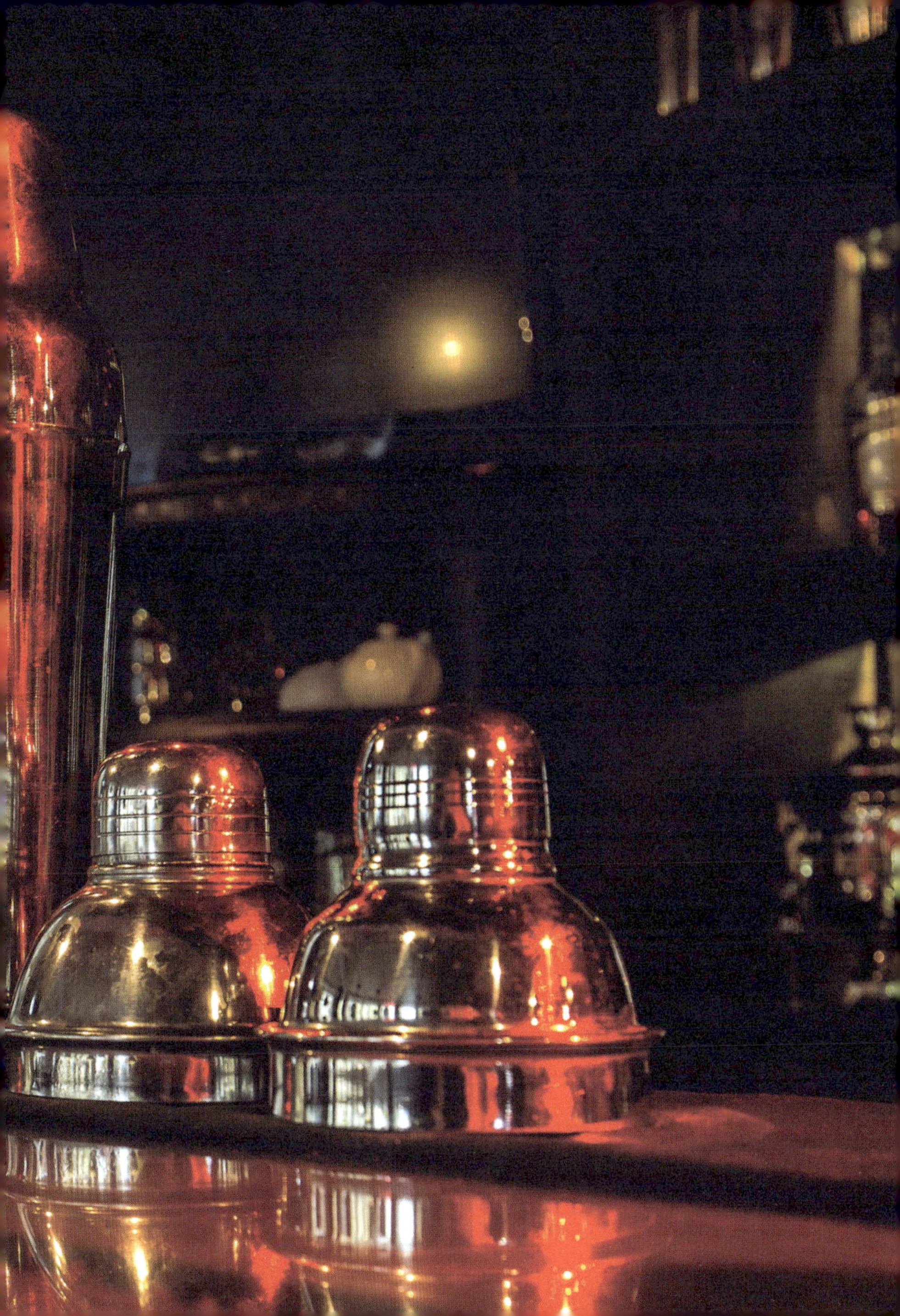

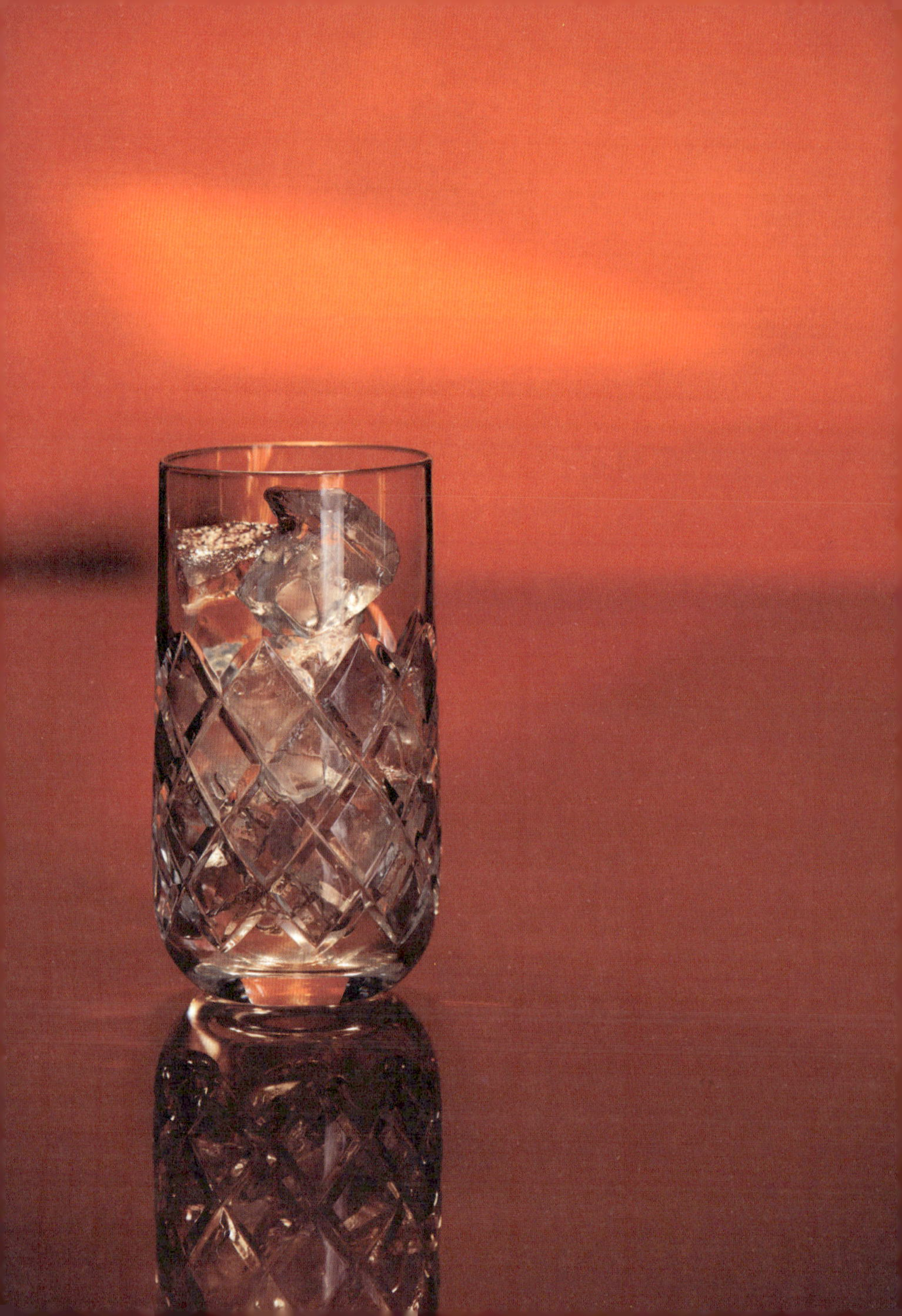

DAIQUIRI BLOSSOM

18.6% alc/vol
0.9 standard drinks

30 ml (1 fl oz) Bacardi
dash maraschino liqueur
30 ml (1 fl oz) fresh orange juice

Pour ingredients into a cocktail shaker over ice and shake. Strain into a chilled cocktail glass and serve with a short orange straw.

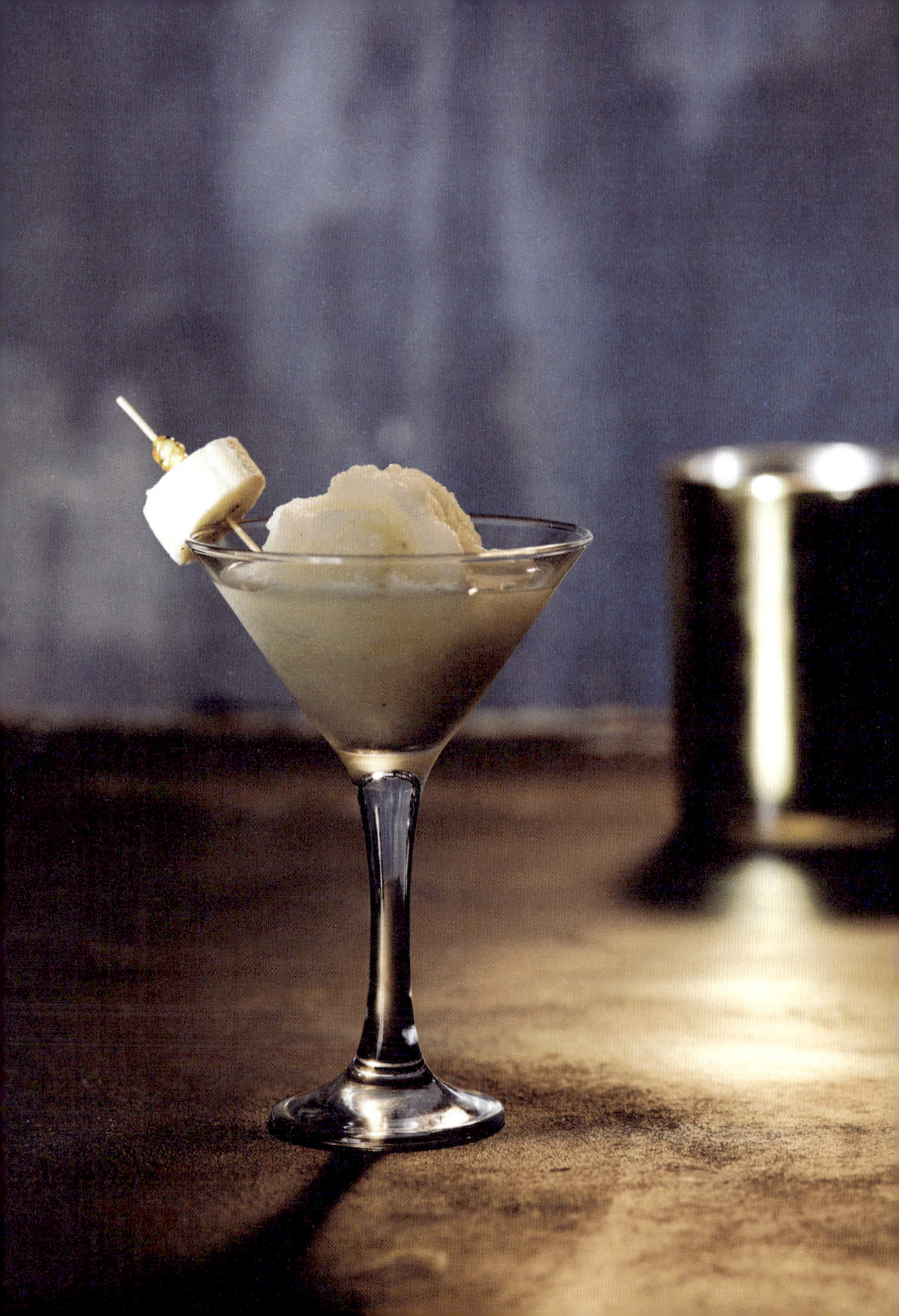

BANANA DAIQUIRI

14.2% alc/vol
1.2 standard drinks

30 ml (1 fl oz) Bacardi
15 ml (½ fl oz) banana liqueur
30 ml (1 fl oz) fresh lemon juice
½ fresh banana (diced)
slice of fresh banana

Pour Bacardi, liqueur and juice into a blender over a small amount of crushed ice then add diced banana. Blend until smooth and pour into a chilled cocktail glass. Garnish with a slice of banana and serve.

DAIQUIRI NACIONAL

25.9% alc/vol
2.2 standard drinks

45 ml (1½ fl oz) Bacardi
45 ml (1½ fl oz) apricot brandy
15 ml (½ fl oz) fresh lime juice
1 teaspoon sugar syrup

Pour ingredients into a blender over a small amount of crushed ice and blend until smooth. Pour into a chilled cocktail glass and serve with a short orange straw.

DERBY DAIQUIRI

18% alc/vol
1.3 standard drinks

45 ml (1½ fl oz) Bacardi
30 ml (1 fl oz) fresh orange juice
15 ml (½ fl oz) fresh lime juice
1 teaspoon sugar syrup

Pour ingredients into a cocktail shaker over ice and shake well. Strain into a chilled cocktail glass and serve with a short orange straw.

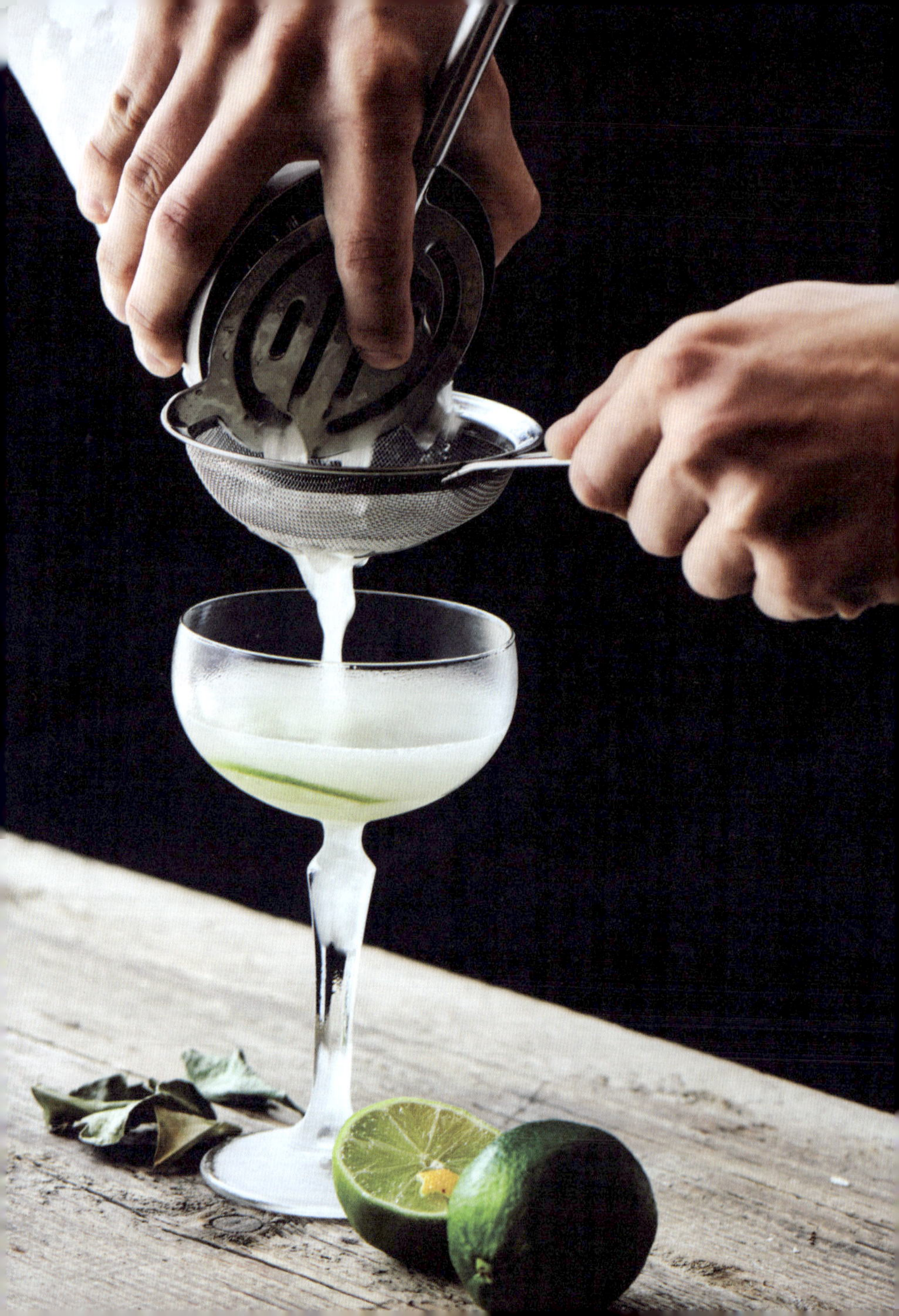

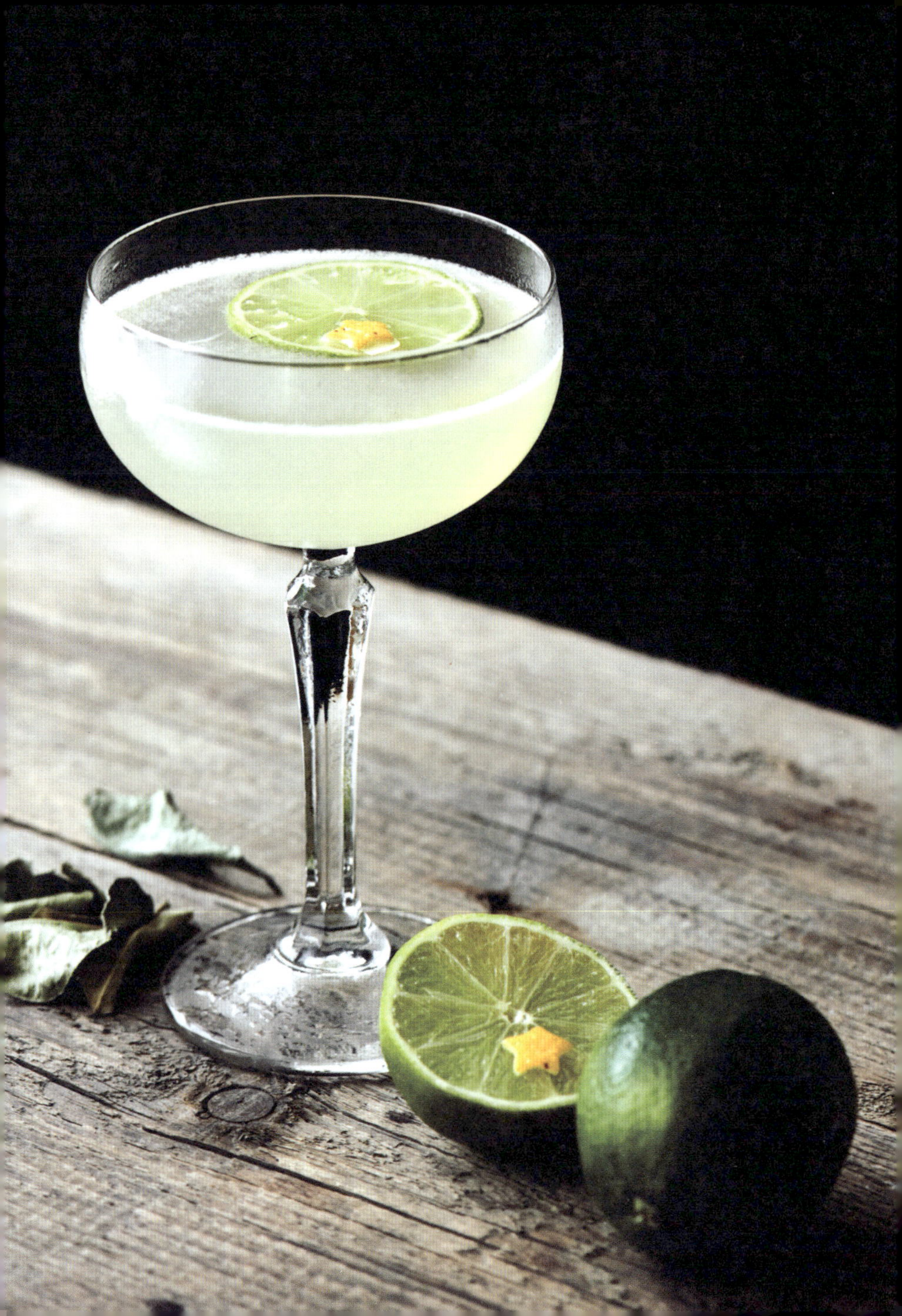

PEACH DAIQUIRI

11.4% alc/vol
1.6 standard drinks

45 ml (1½ fl oz) Bacardi
15 ml (½ fl oz) peach liqueur
30 ml (1 fl oz) fresh lemon juice
1 fresh peach (diced)
slice of fresh peach

Pour Bacardi, liqueur and juice into a blender over a small amount of crushed ice then add diced peach. Blend until smooth and pour into a chilled cocktail glass. Garnish with a slice of peach and serve with a short orange straw.

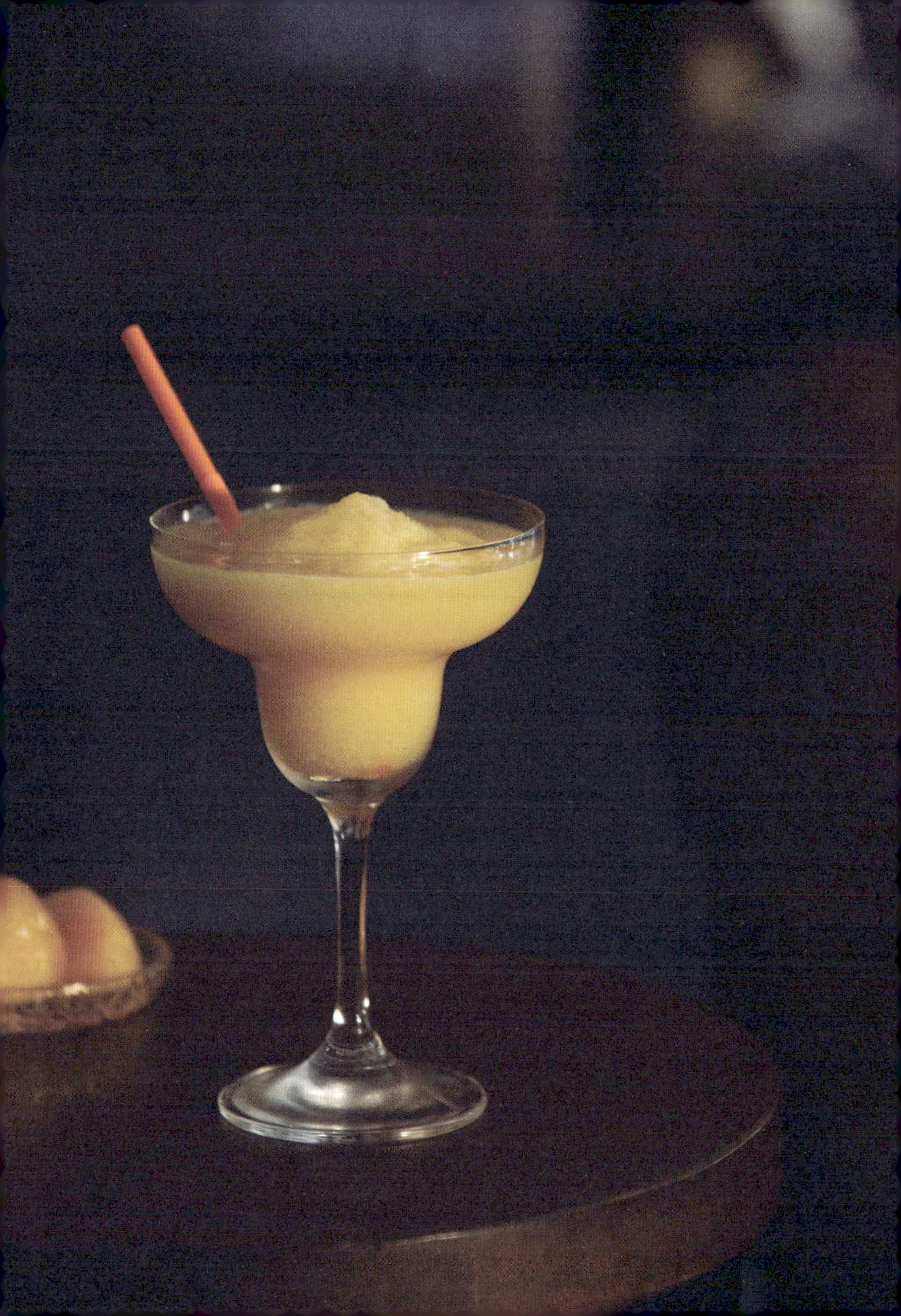

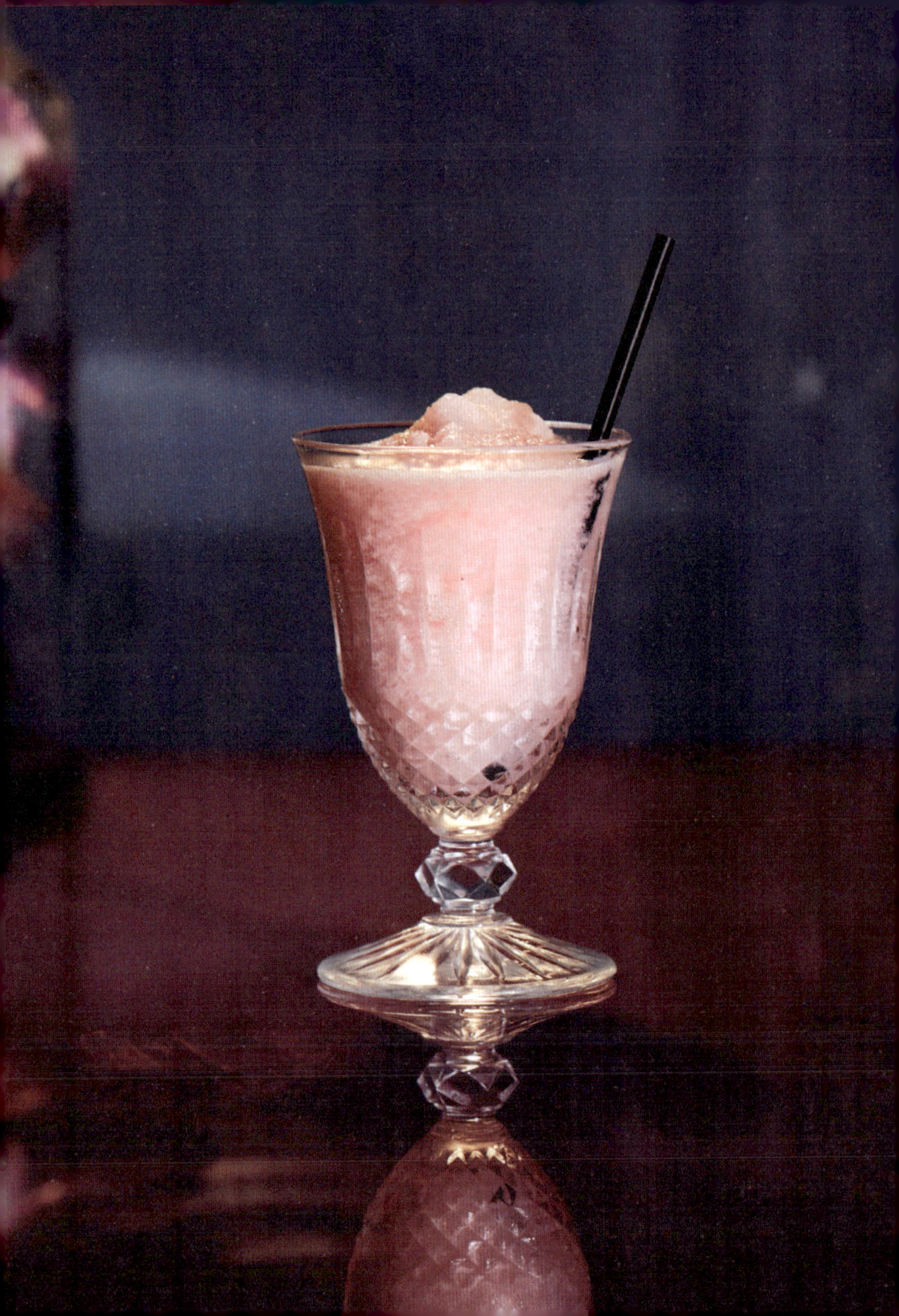

LA FLORIDA DAIQUIRI

23.5% alc/vol
1.9 standard drinks

60 ml (2 fl oz) Bacardi
5 ml (⅙ fl oz) Grenadine
30 ml (1 fl oz) fresh lime juice
1 teaspoon sugar syrup

Pour ingredients into a blender over a small amount of crushed ice and blend until smooth. Pour into a chilled cocktail glass and serve with a straw.

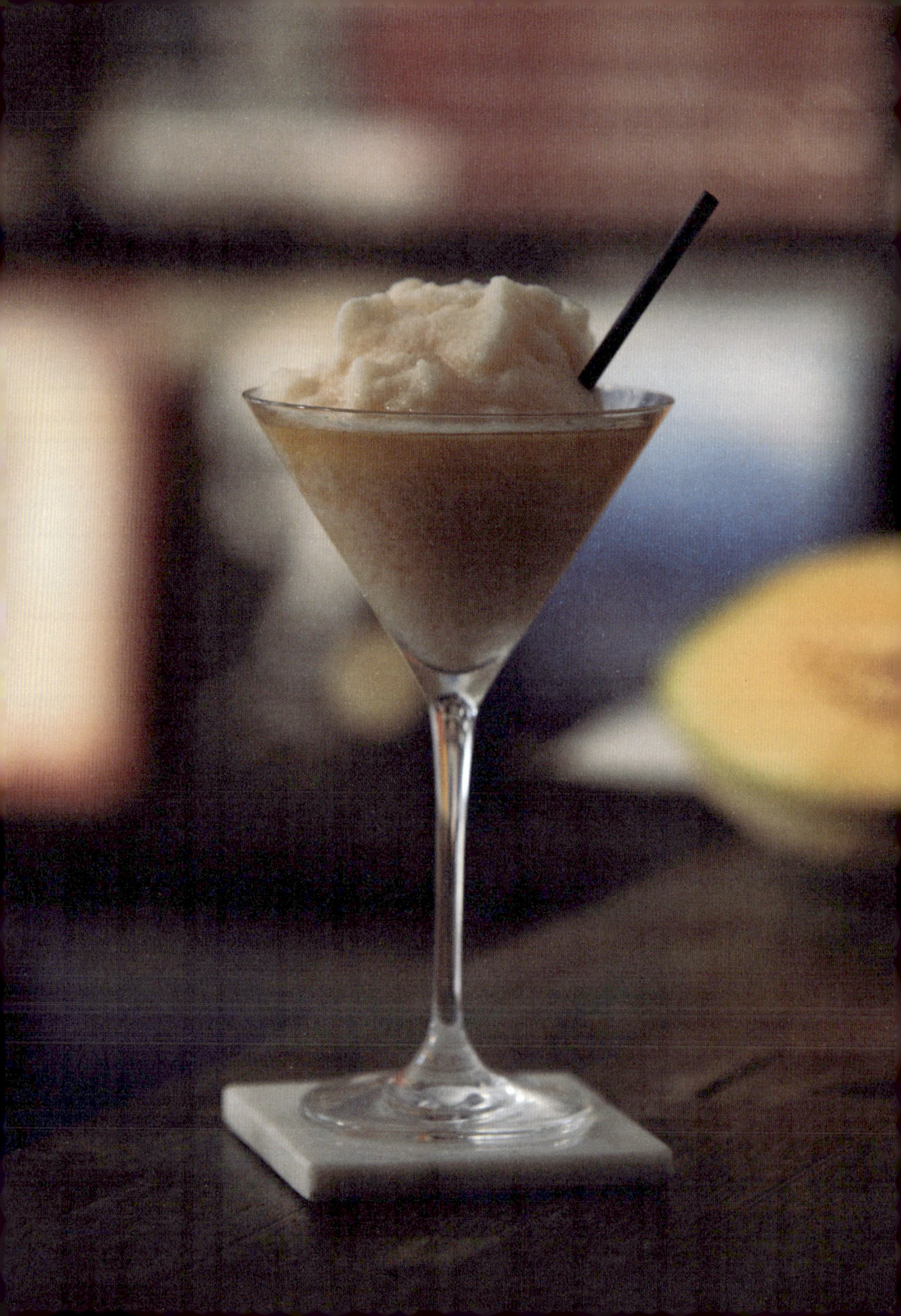

ROCKMELON DAIQUIRI

11.9% alc/vol
2.6 standard drinks

45 ml (1½ fl oz) Bacardi
30 ml (1 fl oz) Cointreau
20 ml (⅔ fl oz) mango liqueur
20 ml (⅔ fl oz) fresh lemon juice
⅓ fresh rockmelon (diced)

Pour Bacardi, Cointreau, liqueur and juice into a blender over a small amount of crushed ice then add diced rockmelon. Blend until smooth and pour into a chilled cocktail glass then serve with a short straw.

BANANA DAIQUIRI NO.2

13.4% alc/vol
1.8 standard drinks

45 ml (1½ fl oz) Bacardi
15 ml (½ fl oz) Cointreau
45 ml (1½ fl oz) fresh lime juice
1 teaspoon sugar syrup
1 fresh banana (diced)
maraschino cherry
slice of fresh banana

Pour Bacardi, Cointreau, juice and sugar into a blender over a small amount of crushed ice then add diced banana. Blend until smooth and pour into a chilled cocktail glass. Garnish with a maraschino cherry and a slice of banana then serve with a short yellow straw.

CHAMBORD DAIQUIRI

18.8% alc/vol
1 standard drink

23 ml (¾ fl oz) Bacardi
23 ml (¾ fl oz) Chambord
15 ml (½ fl oz) fresh lemon juice
1 teaspoon sugar syrup

Pour ingredients into a blender over a small amount of crushed ice and blend until smooth. Pour into a chilled cocktail glass and serve with a short red straw.

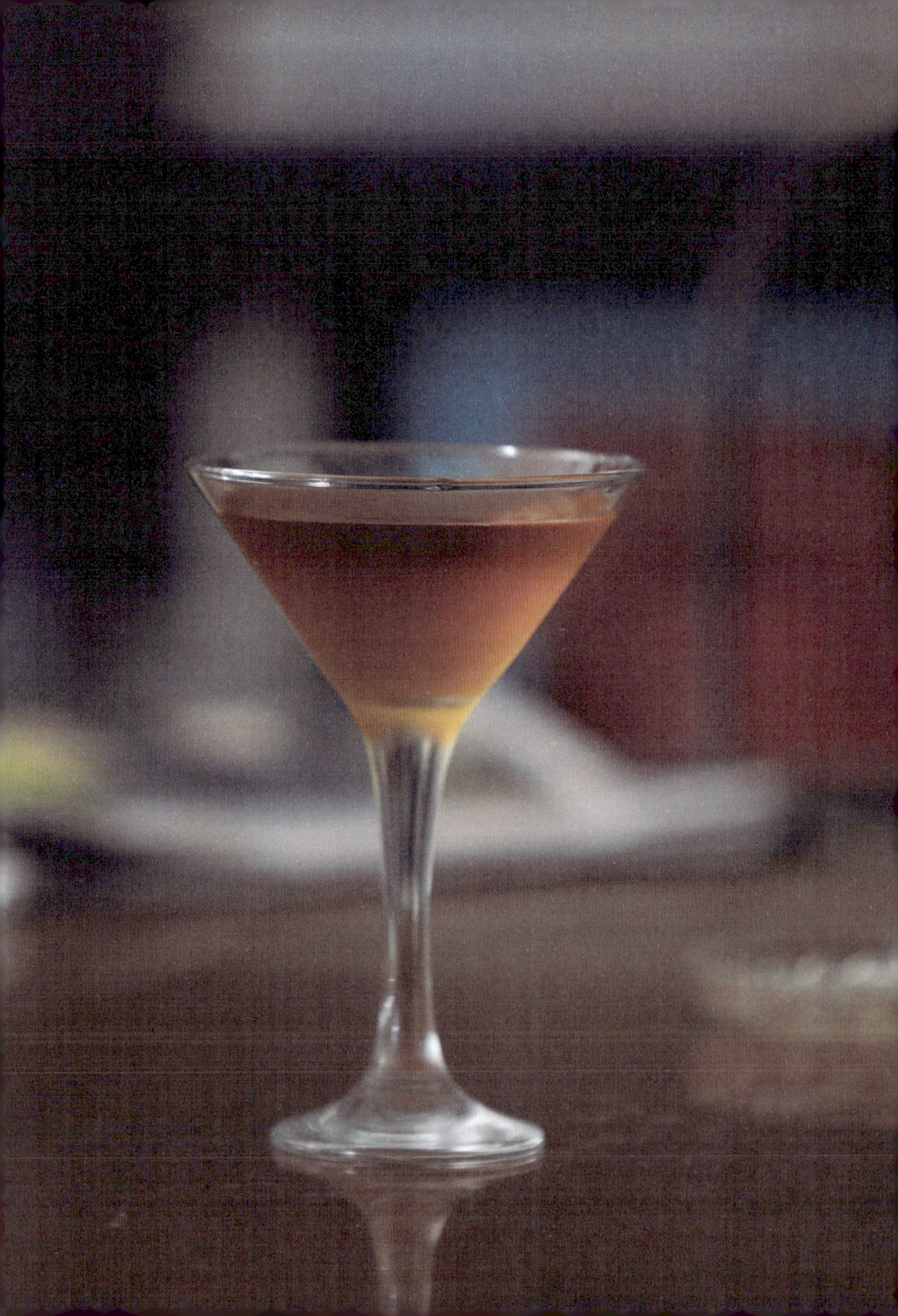

DAIQUIRI LIBERAL

29.7% alc/vol
2.1 standard drinks

60 ml (2 fl oz) Bacardi
30 ml (1 fl oz) sweet vermouth
dash Amer Picon

Pour ingredients into a mixing glass over ice and stir. Strain into a chilled cocktail glass and serve.

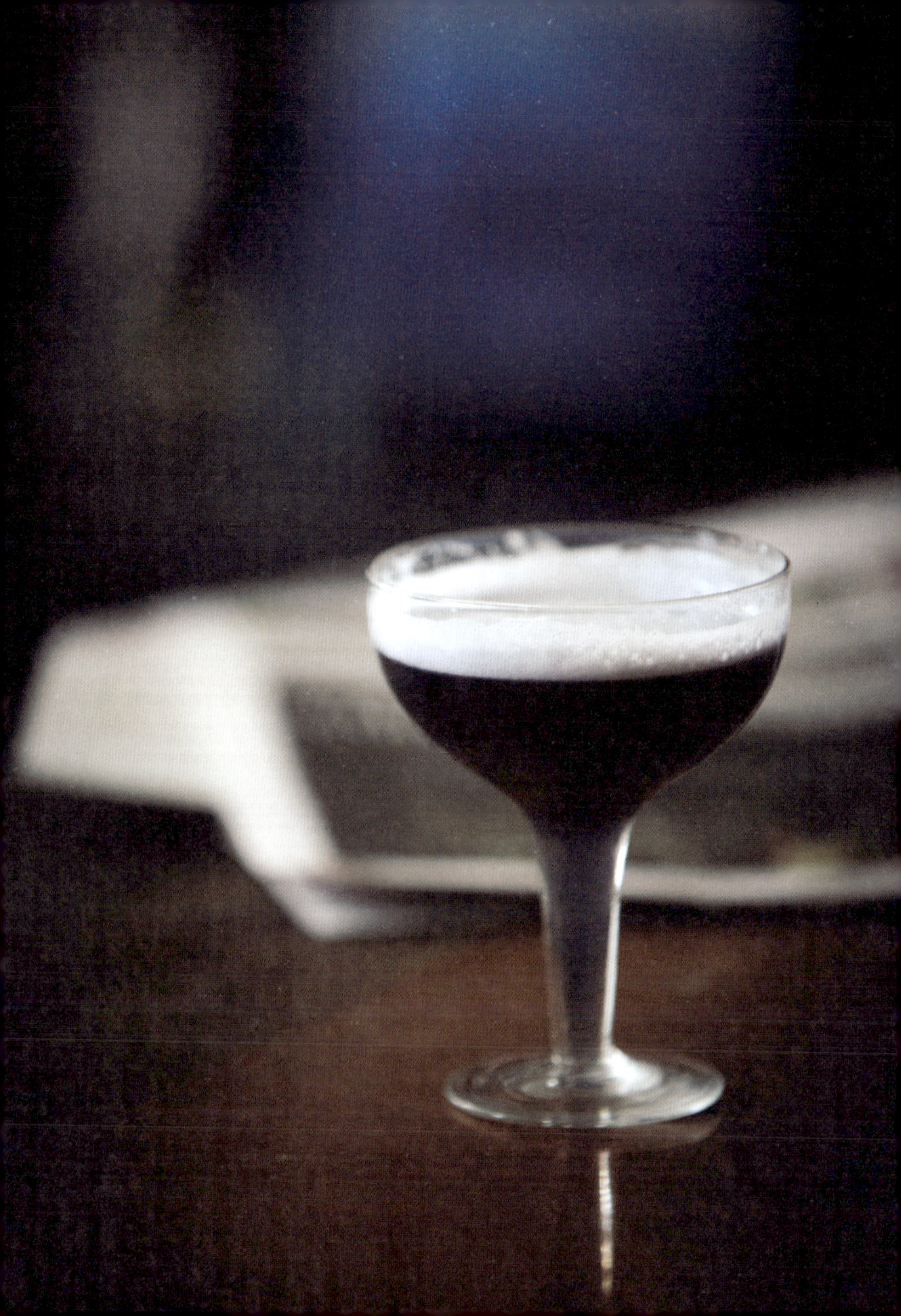

KING'S DAIQUIRI

22.3% alc/vol
1.3 standard drinks

15 ml (½ fl oz) Bacardi
15 ml (½ fl oz) Cointreau
15 ml (½ fl oz) Parfait Amour
15 ml (½ fl oz) fresh lemon juice
1 teaspoon egg white
½ teaspoon sugar syrup

Pour ingredients into a cocktail shaker over ice and shake well. Strain into a chilled cocktail glass and serve.

BLUEBERRY DAIQUIRI

17.4% alc/vol

1.7 standard drinks

45 ml (1½ fl oz) Bacardi
23 ml (¾ fl oz) blueberry schnapps
15 ml (½ fl oz) fresh lemon juice
1 teaspoon sugar syrup
4 fresh blueberries (diced)

Pour Bacardi, schnapps, juice and sugar into a blender over a small amount of crushed ice then add diced blueberries. Blend until smooth and pour into a chilled cocktail glass. Garnish with a fresh blueberry if desired and serve.

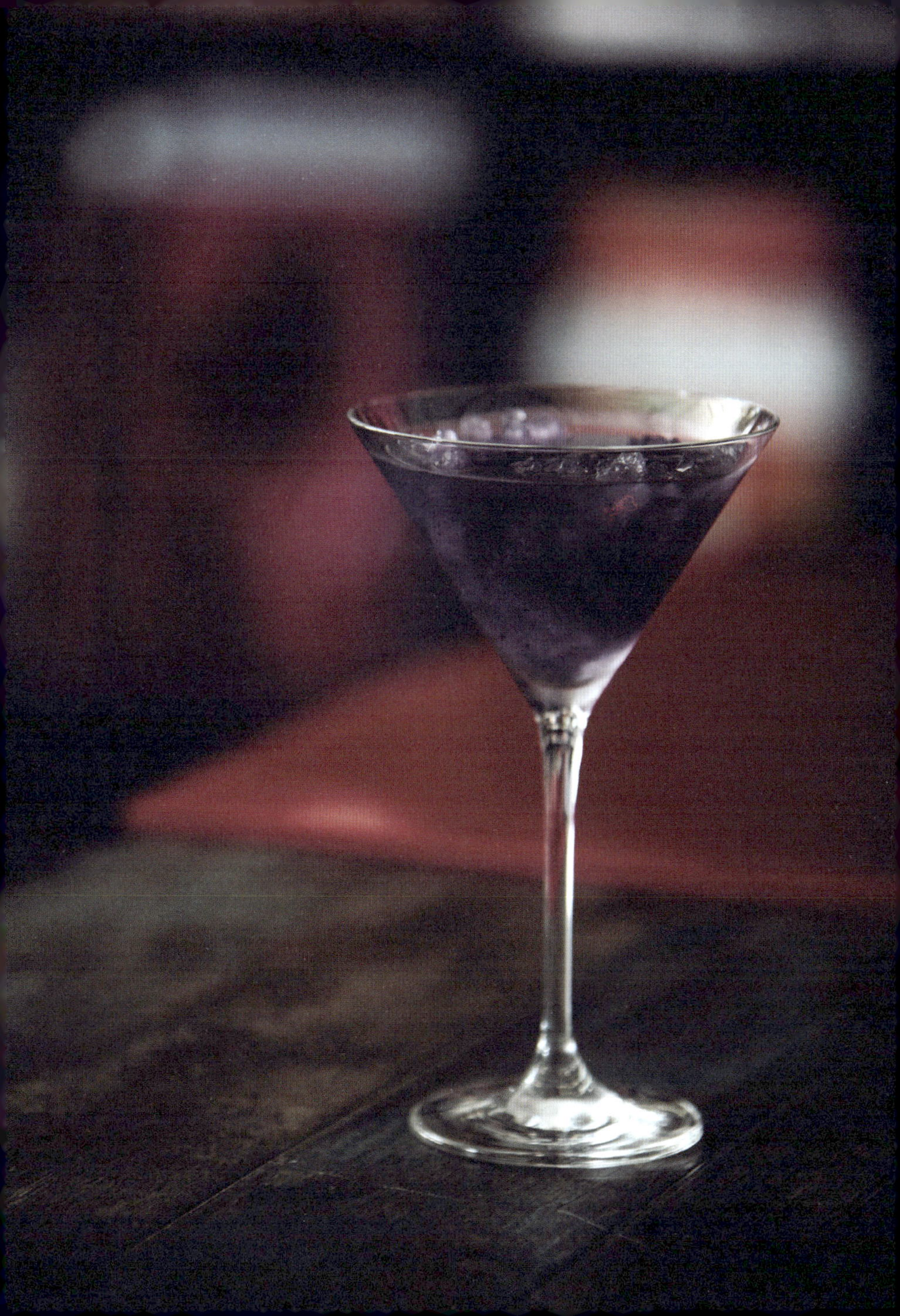

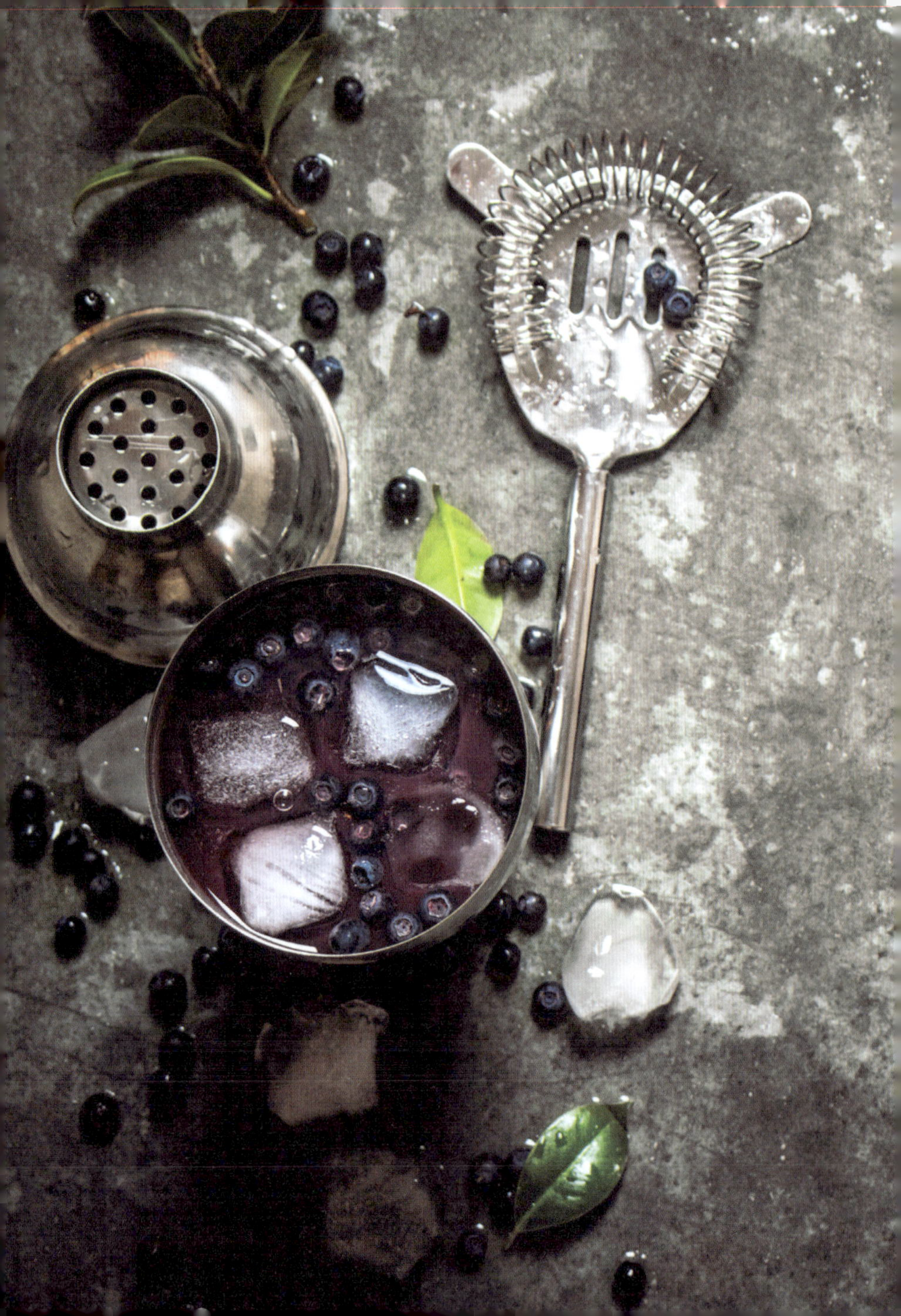

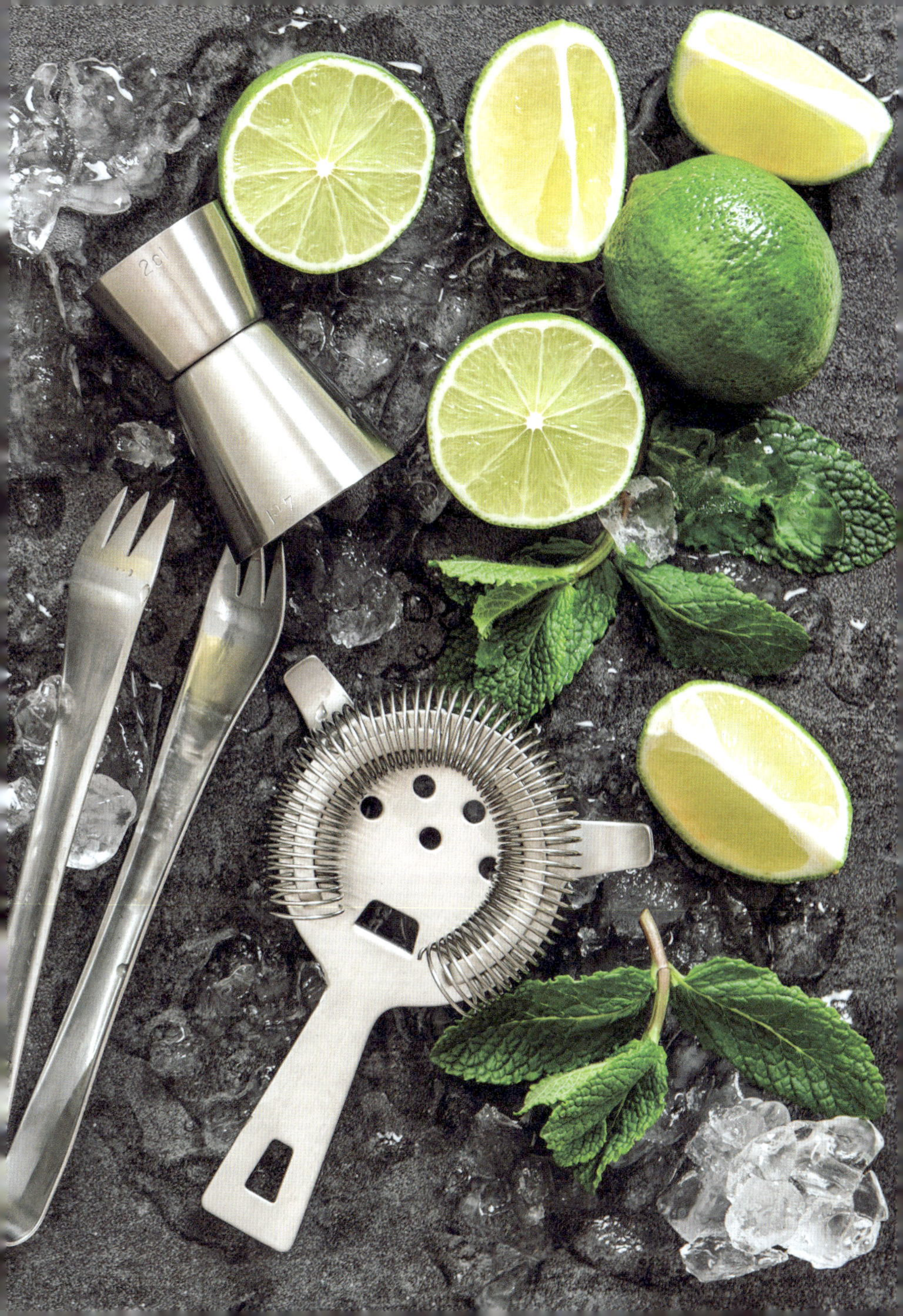

DAIQUIRI COCKTAIL

21.1% alc/vol
1.3 standard drinks

45 ml (1½ fl oz) Bacardi
30 ml (1 fl oz) fresh lime juice
1 teaspoon sugar syrup

Pour ingredients into a cocktail shaker over ice and shake. Strain into a chilled cocktail glass and serve with a short green straw.

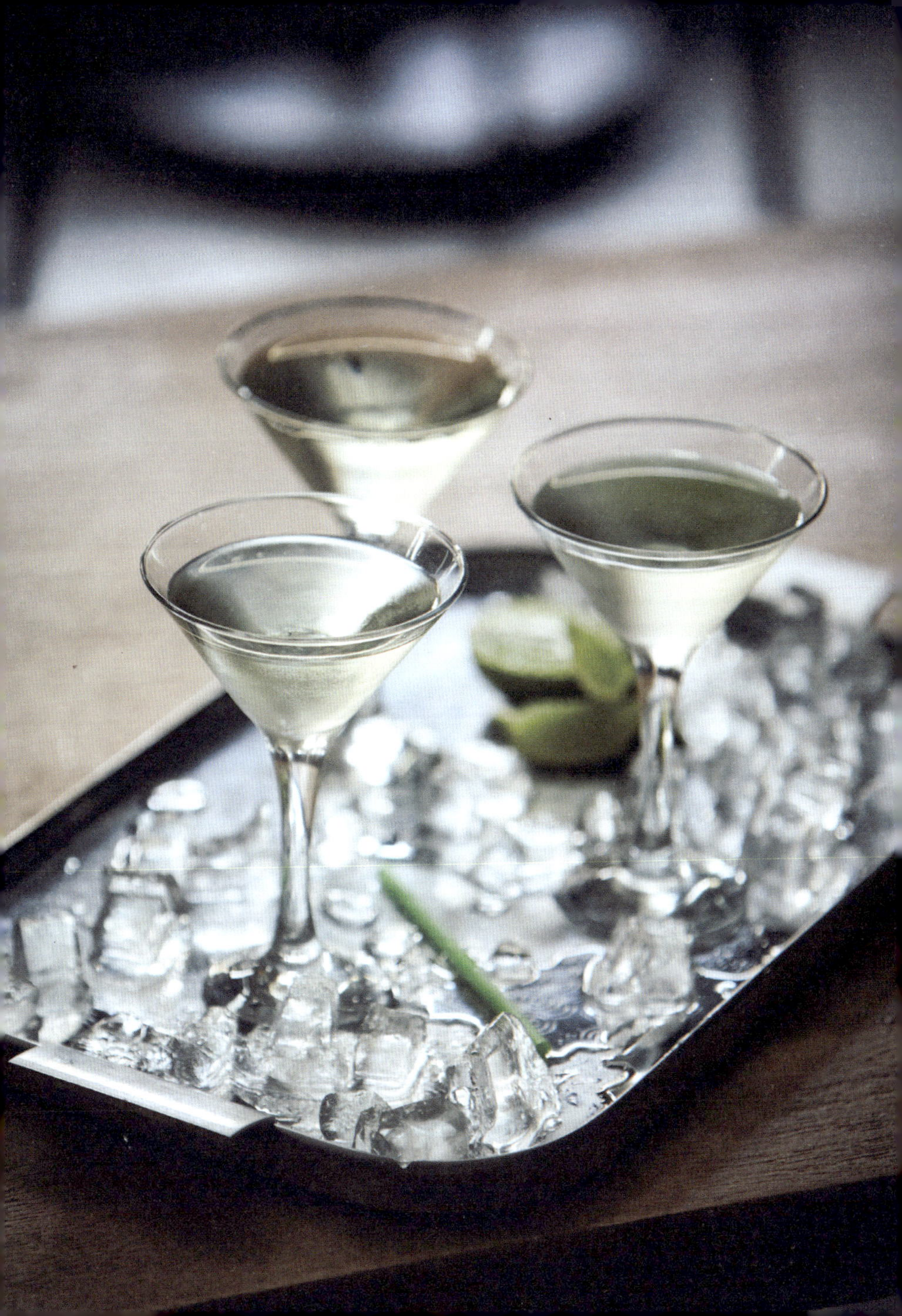

FROZEN SESAME DAIQUIRI

18.9% alc/vol

1.6 standard drinks

45 ml (1½ fl oz) Bacardi
15 ml (½ fl oz) dry vermouth
15 ml (½ fl oz) fresh lime juice
15 ml (½ fl oz) fresh orange juice
15 ml (½ fl oz) sesame-seed syrup

Pour ingredients into a blender over a large amount of crushed ice and blend until slushy. Pour into a frosted cocktail glass and serve with a short orange straw.

FROZEN GUAVA-ORANGE DAIQUIRI

17.4% alc/vol
1.3 standard drinks

45 ml (1½ fl oz) Bacardi
23 ml (¾ fl oz) guava syrup
15 ml (½ fl oz) fresh lime juice
15 ml (½ fl oz) fresh orange juice

Pour ingredients into a blender over a large amount of crushed ice and blend until slushy. Pour into a frosted cocktail glass and serve with a short orange straw.

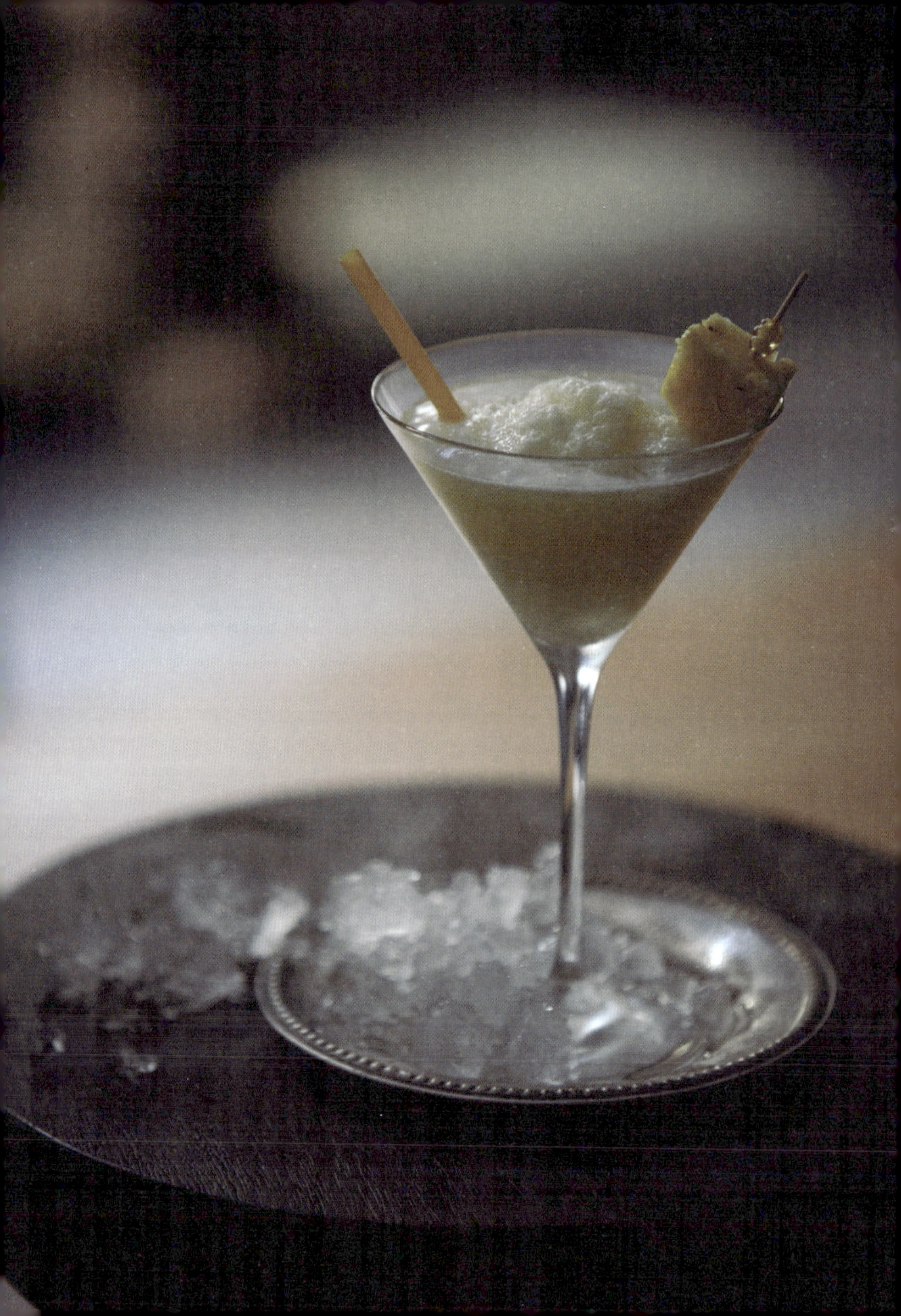

PINEAPPLE DAIQUIRI

21.4% alc/vol
2.2 standard drinks

60 ml (2 fl oz) Bacardi
15 ml (½ fl oz) Cointreau
15 ml (½ fl oz) fresh lemon juice
15 ml (½ fl oz) fresh lime juice
6 pieces of fresh pineapple (diced)
slice of fresh pineapple

Pour Bacardi, Cointreau and juices into a blender over a small amount of crushed ice then add diced pineapple. Blend until smooth and pour into a chilled cocktail glass. Garnish with a slice of pineapple and serve with a short yellow straw.

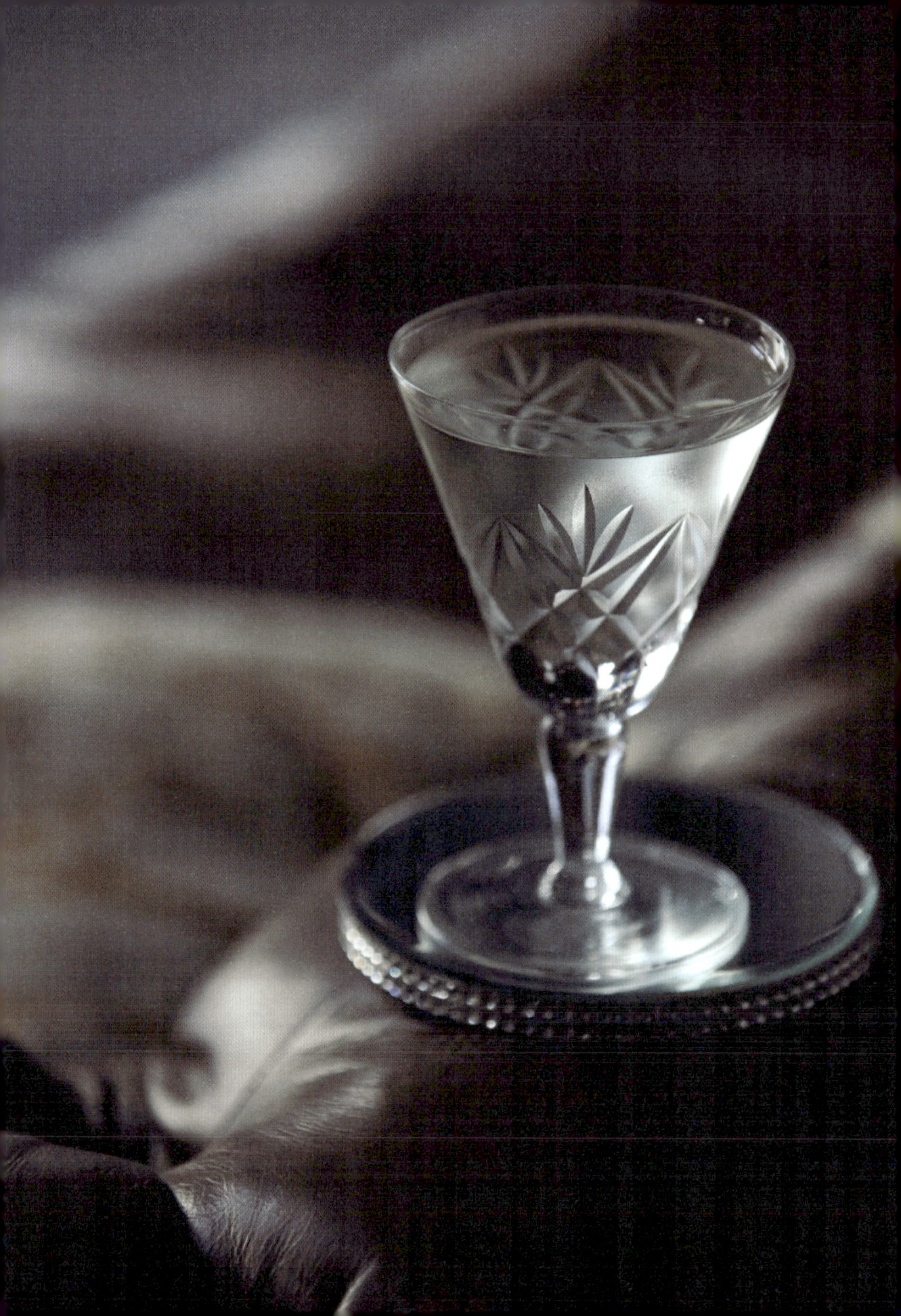

LIME DAIQUIRI

26.4% alc/vol
2 standard drinks

45 ml (1½ fl oz) Bacardi
20 ml (⅔ fl oz) Cointreau
30 ml (1 fl oz) fresh lime juice

Pour ingredients into a cocktail shaker over ice and shake well. Strain into a chilled cocktail glass and serve.

ORANGE DAIQUIRI

16.3% alc/vol
1.8 standard drinks

60 ml (2 fl oz) Bacardi
60 ml (2 fl oz) fresh orange juice
15 ml (½ fl oz) fresh lime juice
1 teaspoon sugar syrup
slice of fresh orange

Pour Bacardi, juices and sugar into a cocktail shaker over ice then shake well. Strain into a chilled cocktail glass and garnish with a slice of orange if desired then serve.

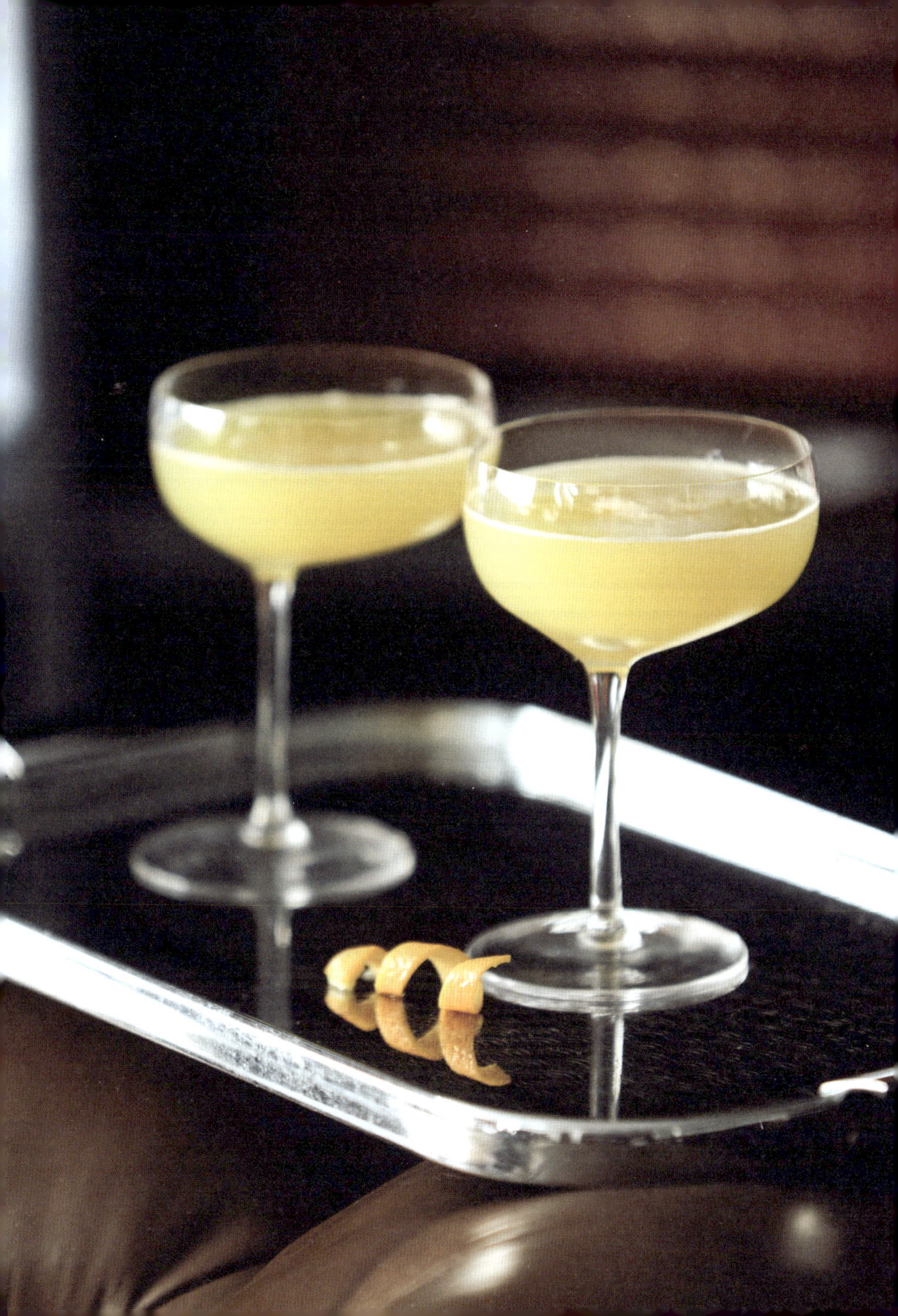

PASSION DAIQUIRI

18.5% alc/vol
1.8 standard drinks

60 ml (2 fl oz) Bacardi
30 ml (1 fl oz) fresh lime juice
30 ml (1 fl oz) passionfruit juice
½ teaspoon sugar syrup

Pour ingredients into a cocktail shaker over ice and shake well. Strain into a chilled cocktail glass and serve.

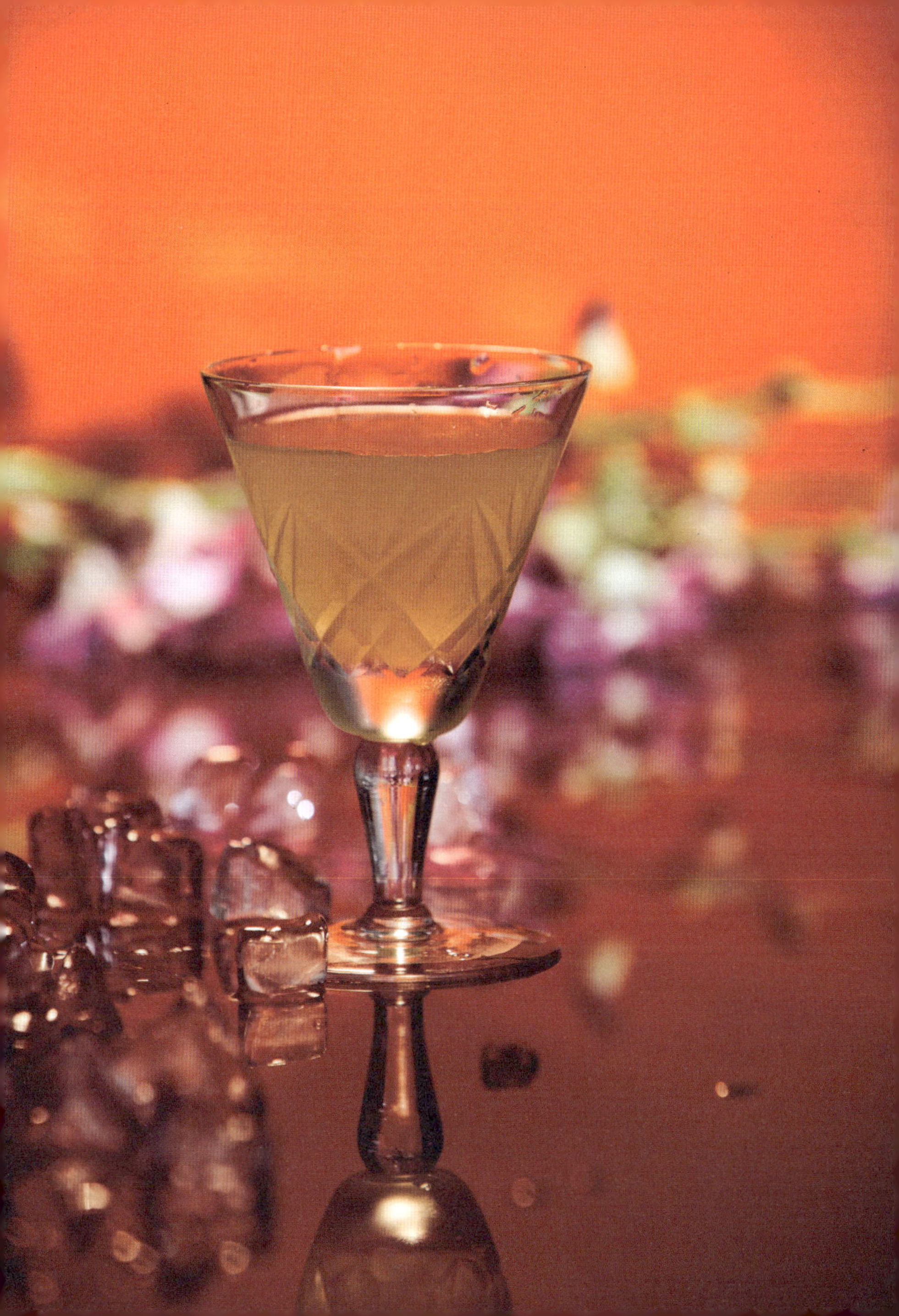

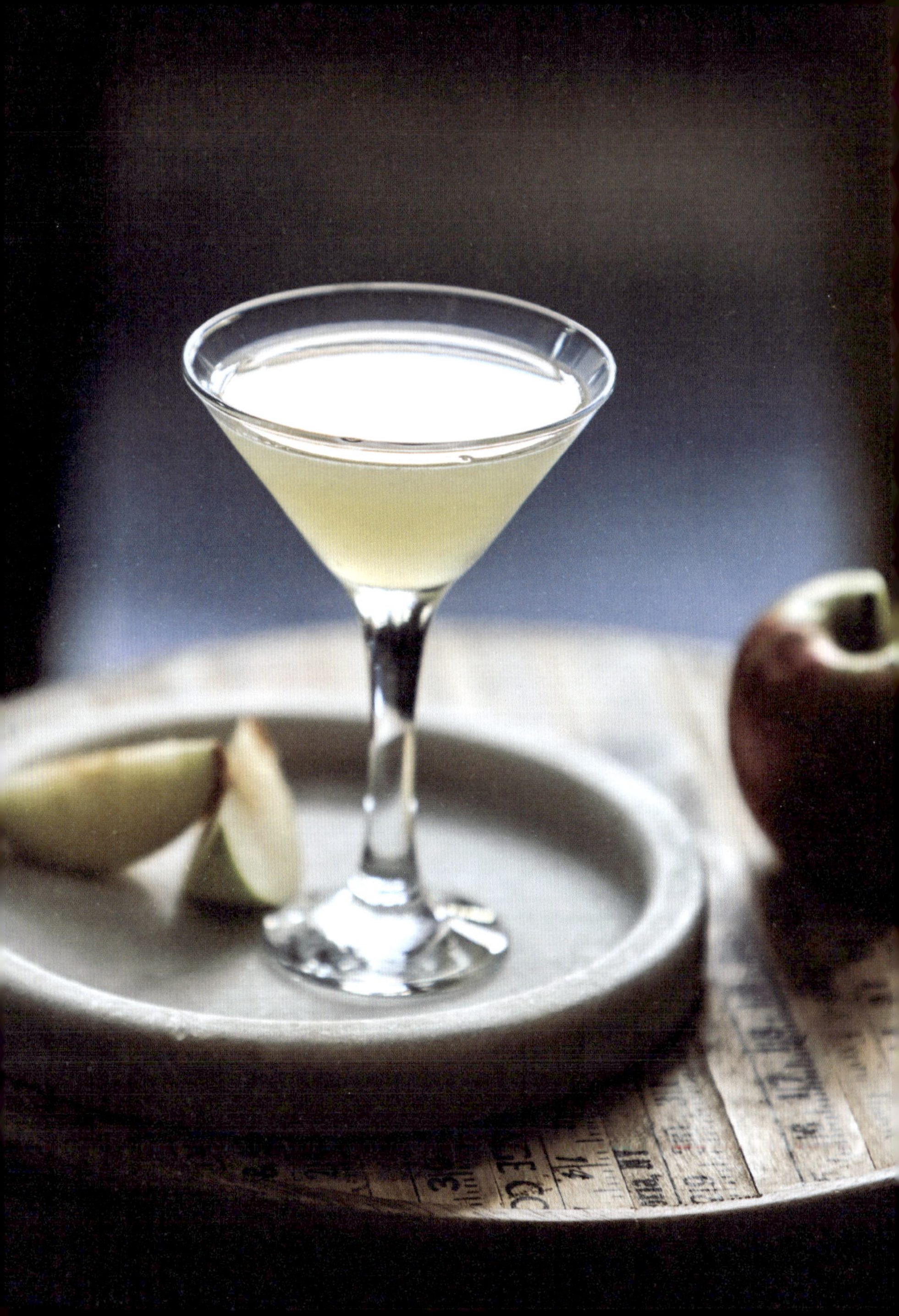

APPLE DAIQUIRI

21.1% alc/vol
1.3 standard drinks

45 ml (1½ fl oz) Bacardi
15 ml (½ fl oz) apple juice
15 ml (½ fl oz) fresh lime juice
1 teaspoon sugar syrup

Pour ingredients into a cocktail shaker over ice and shake. Strain into a chilled cocktail glass and serve.

FRENCH DAIQUIRI

20.8% alc/vol
0.6 standard drinks

20 ml (⅔ fl oz) Bacardi
dash Crème de Cassis
15 ml (½ fl oz) fresh lime juice
dash sugar syrup
sprig of fresh mint

Pour Bacardi, Crème de Cassis, juice and sugar into a cocktail shaker over ice then shake. Strain into a chilled cocktail glass and garnish with a sprig of mint then serve with a short red straw.

COCONUT DAIQUIRI

20.9% alc/vol
1.9 standard drinks

45 ml (1½ fl oz) Bacardi
30 ml (1 fl oz) coconut liqueur
30 ml (1 fl oz) fresh lime juice
1 teaspoon sugar syrup
1 teaspoon egg white

Pour ingredients into a cocktail shaker over ice and shake well. Strain into a chilled cocktail glass and serve with a short white straw.

KIWI DAIQUIRI

19.1% alc/vol
1.6 standard drinks

30 ml (1 fl oz) Bacardi
15 ml (½ fl oz) Cointreau
15 ml (½ fl oz) Midori
15 ml (½ fl oz) fresh lime juice
½ teaspoon sugar syrup
½ fresh kiwifruit (diced)
slice of fresh kiwifruit

Pour Bacardi, Cointreau, Midori, juice and sugar into a blender over a small amount of crushed ice then add diced kiwifruit. Blend until smooth and pour into a chilled cocktail glass. Garnish with a slice of kiwifruit and serve with a short green straw.

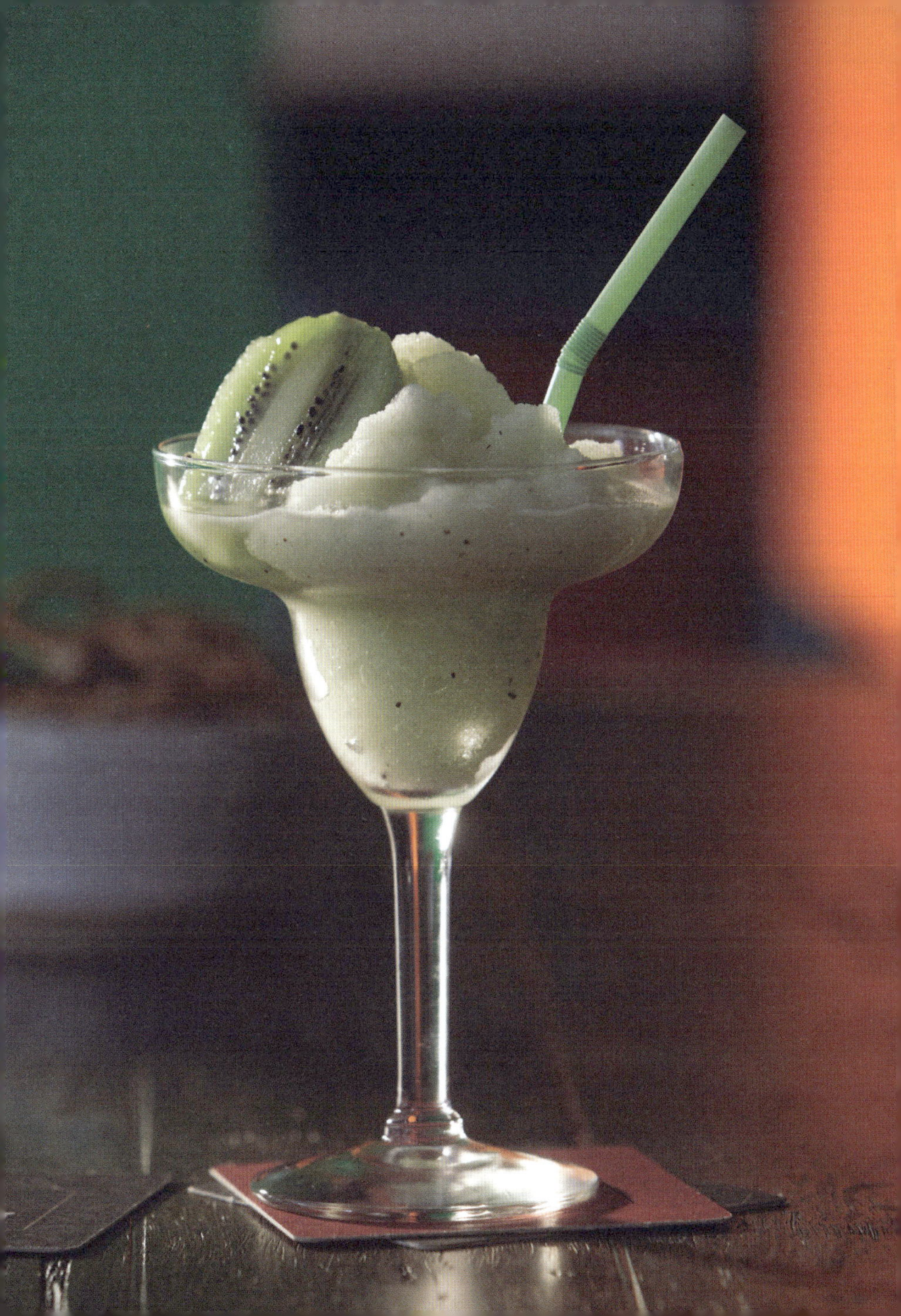

MANDARIN DAIQUIRI

29.3% alc/vol
2 standard drinks

45 ml (1½ fl oz) Bacardi
23 ml (¾ fl oz) Mandarine Napoleon
15 ml (½ fl oz) fresh lime juice
1 teaspoon sugar syrup
maraschino cherry
slice of fresh orange

Pour Bacardi, Mandarine Napoleon, juice and sugar into a blender over a small amount of crushed ice. Blend until smooth and pour into a chilled cocktail glass. Garnish with a maraschino cherry and a slice of orange then serve with a short orange straw.

FROZEN APPLE DAIQUIRI

21.4% alc/vol
1.4 standard drinks

45 ml (1½ fl oz) Bacardi
15 ml (½ fl oz) apple juice
15 ml (½ fl oz) fresh lemon juice
1 teaspoon sugar syrup
wedge of fresh red apple

Pour Bacardi, juices and sugar into a blender over a large amount of crushed ice then blend until slushy. Pour into a frosted cocktail glass and add a wedge of red apple then serve with a short red straw.

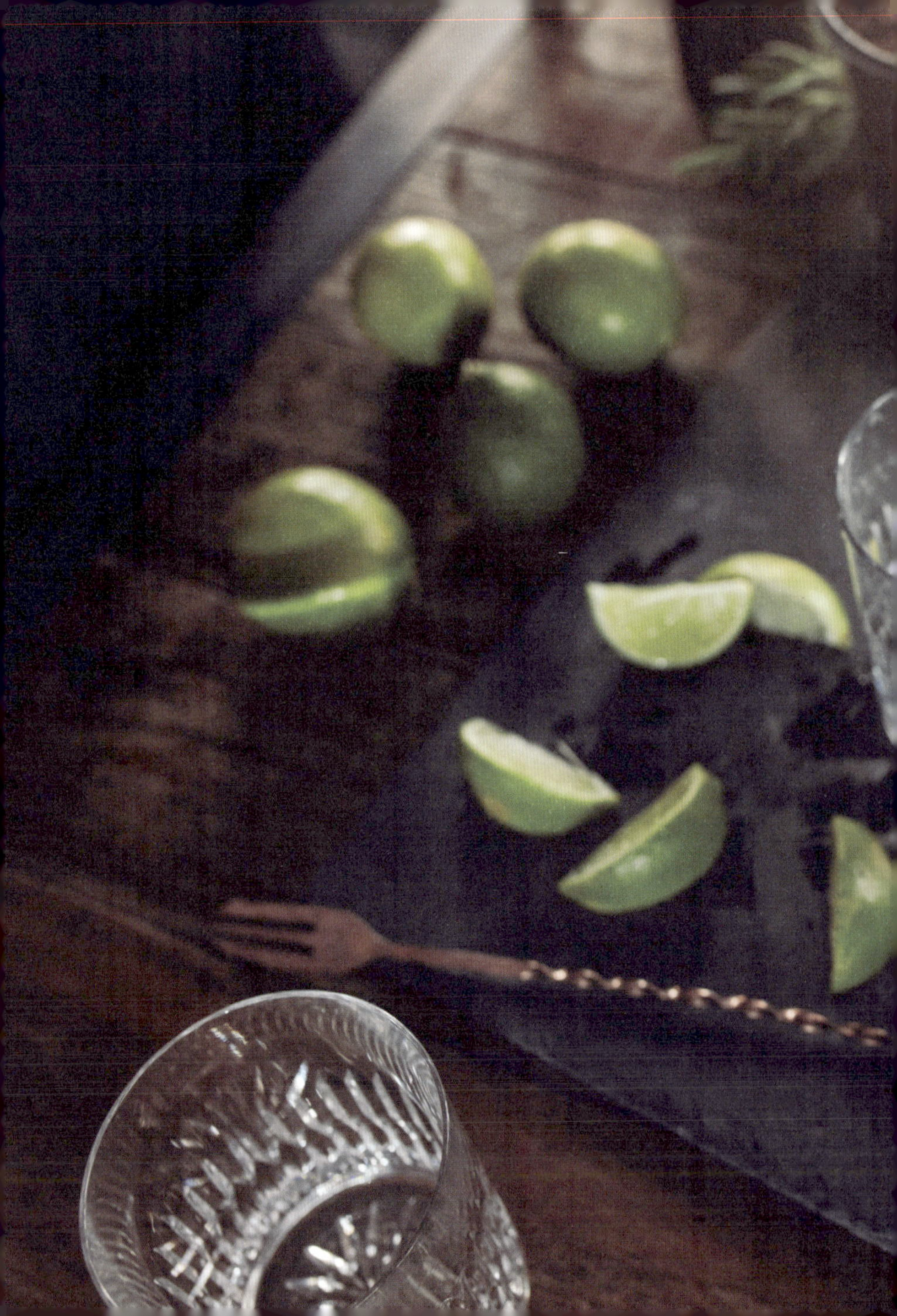

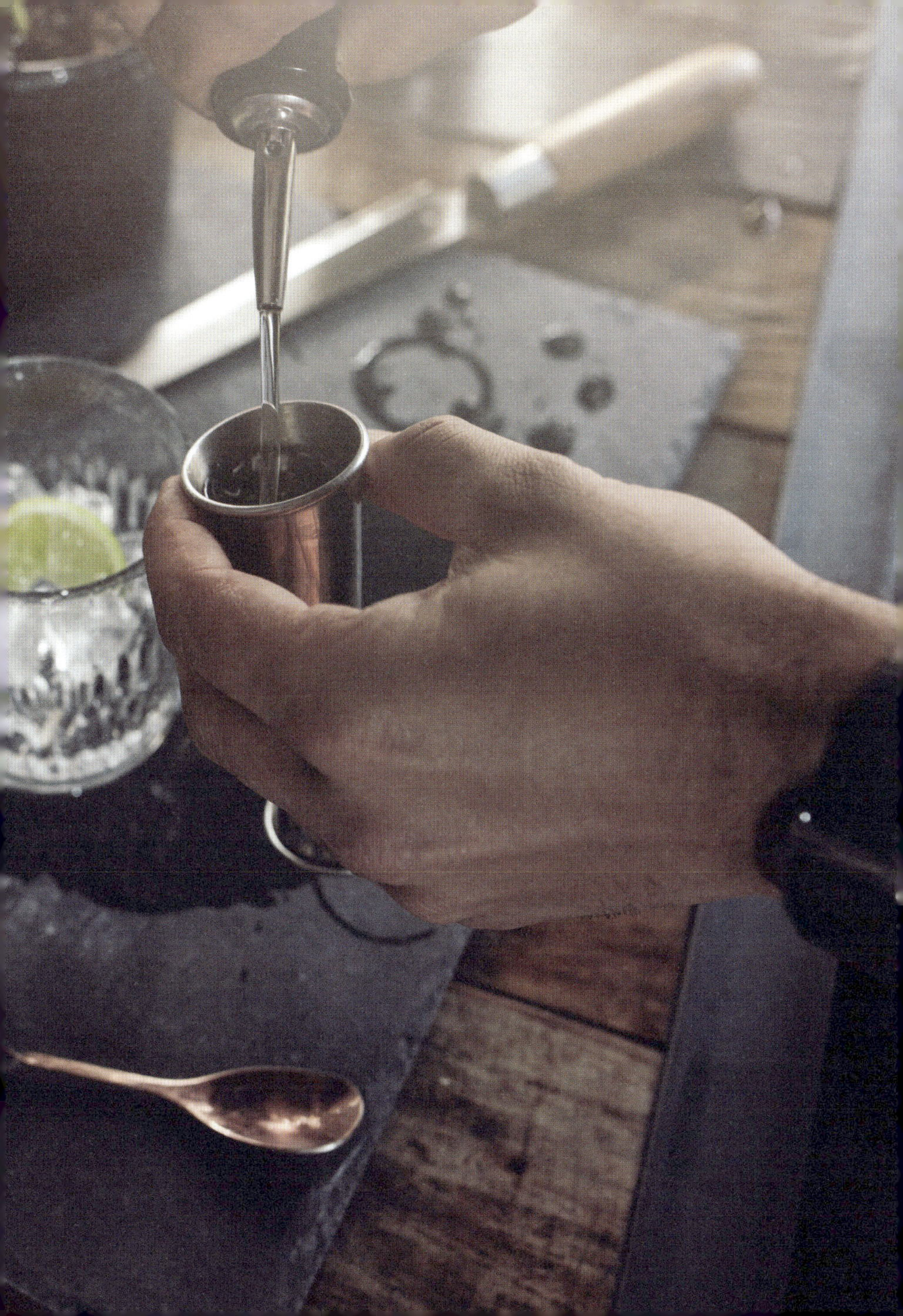

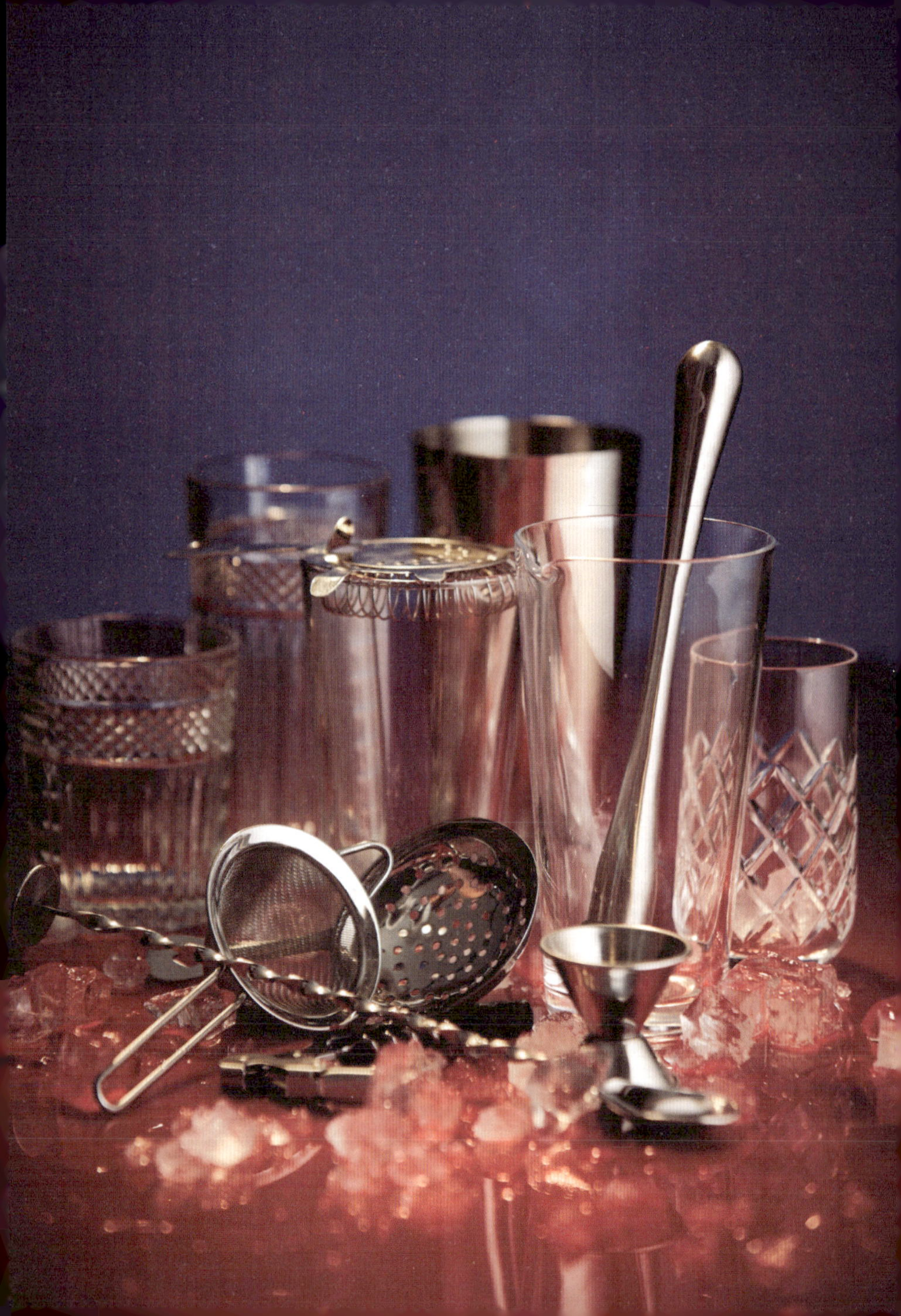

FROZEN PINEAPPLE DAIQUIRI

21.5% alc/vol
1.3 standard drinks

45 ml (1½ fl oz) Bacardi
10 ml (⅓ fl oz) fresh lime juice
½ teaspoon sugar syrup
4 pieces of fresh pineapple

Pour Bacardi, juice and sugar into a blender over a large amount of crushed ice then add pieces of pineapple. Blend until slushy and pour into a frosted cocktail glass then serve with a short yellow straw.

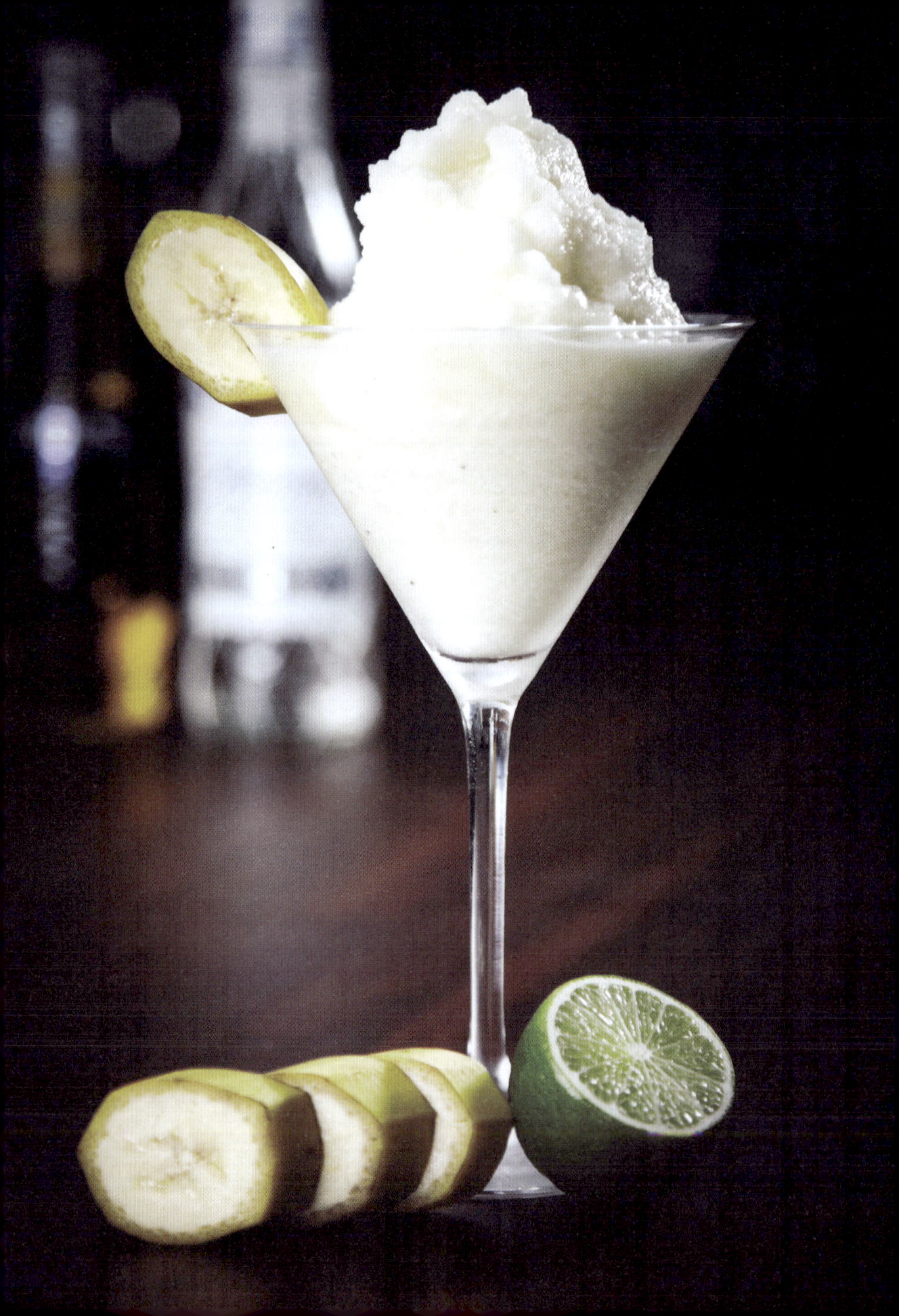

FROZEN BANANA DAIQUIRI

18% alc/vol
1.3 standard drinks

45 ml (1½ fl oz) Bacardi
15 ml (½ fl oz) fresh lime juice
1 teaspoon sugar syrup
½ fresh banana (diced)
slice of fresh banana

Pour Bacardi, juice and sugar into a blender over a large amount of crushed ice then add diced banana. Blend until slushy and pour into a frosted cocktail glass. Garnish with a slice of banana then serve.

FROZEN PASSIONFRUIT DAIQUIRI

17.4% alc/vol
1.3 standard drinks

45 ml (1½ fl oz) Bacardi
15 ml (½ fl oz) fresh lime juice
15 ml (½ fl oz) fresh orange juice
15 ml (½ fl oz) passionfruit syrup
8 ml (¼ fl oz) fresh lemon juice

Pour ingredients into a blender over a large amount of crushed ice and blend until slushy. Pour into a frosted cocktail glass and serve with a short yellow straw.

FROZEN GUAVA DAIQUIRI

19.2% alc/vol
1.4 standard drinks

45 ml (1½ fl oz) Bacardi
5 ml (⅕ fl oz) banana liqueur
30 ml (1 fl oz) guava nectar
15 ml (½ fl oz) fresh lime juice

Pour ingredients into a blender over a large amount of crushed ice and blend until slushy. Pour into a frosted cocktail glass and serve with a short straw.

FROZEN PEACH DAIQUIRI

16.3% alc/vol
1.4 standard drinks

45 ml (1½ fl oz) Bacardi
15 ml (½ fl oz) fresh lime juice
15 ml (½ fl oz) peach syrup
¼ cup fresh peach (diced)

Pour Bacardi, juice and peach syrup into a blender over a large amount of crushed ice then add diced peach. Blend until slushy and pour into a frosted cocktail glass then serve with a short orange straw.

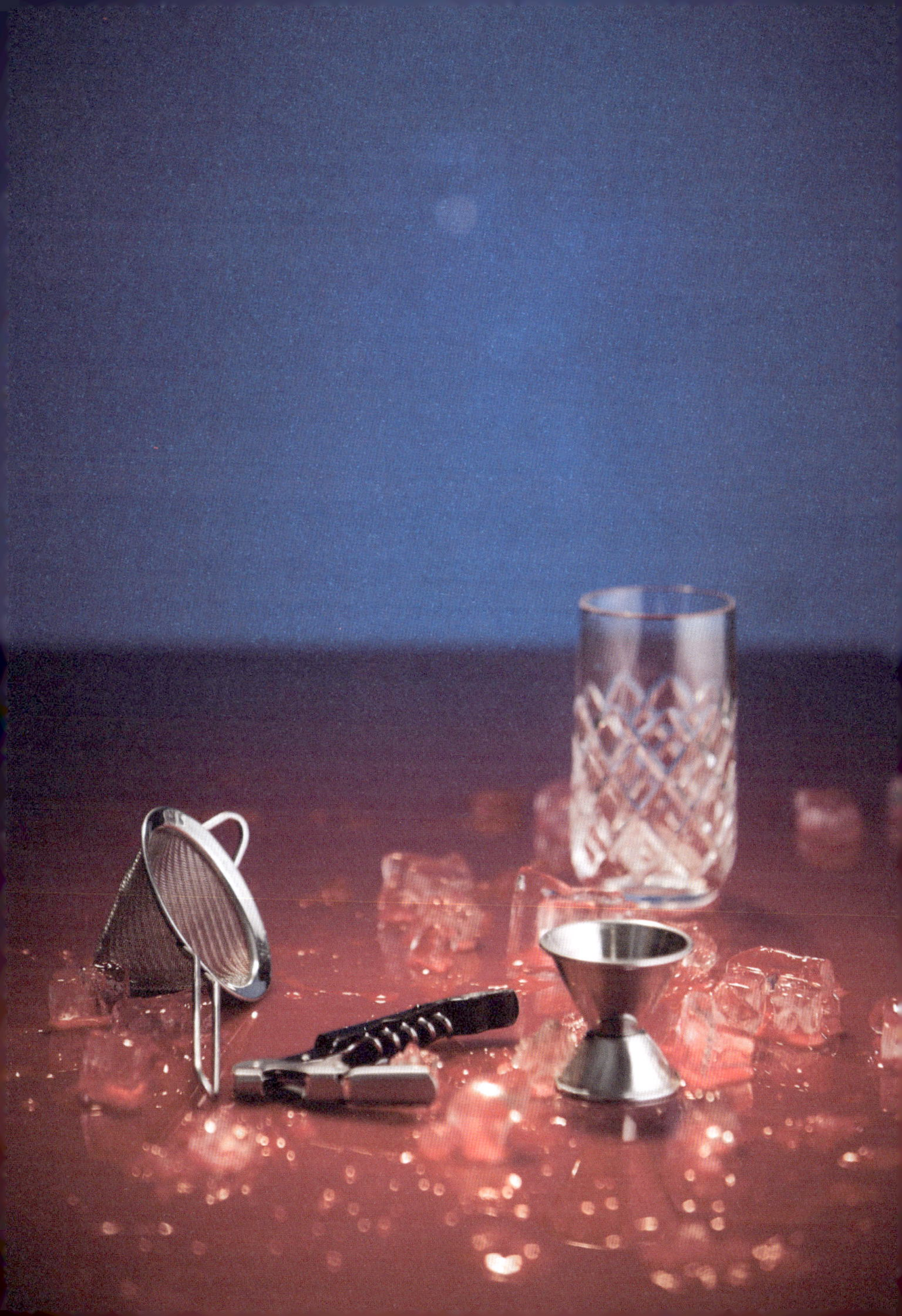

FROZEN SHERRY DAIQUIRI

21.2% alc/vol
1.5 standard drinks

30 ml (1 fl oz) Bacardi
40 ml (1⅓ fl oz) medium-dry sherry
10 ml (⅓ fl oz) fresh lime juice
1½ teaspoons sugar syrup

Pour ingredients into a blender over a large amount of crushed ice and blend until slushy. Pour into a frosted cocktail glass and serve with a short straw.

FROZEN SOURSOP DAIQUIRI

16.5% alc/vol
1.6 standard drinks

45 ml (1½ fl oz) Bacardi
8 ml (¼ fl oz) Jamaican rum
30 ml (1 fl oz) guanabana nectar
8 ml (¼ fl oz) fresh lime juice
½ fresh banana (diced)

Pour Bacardi, rum, nectar and juice into a blender over a large amount of crushed ice then add diced banana. Blend until slushy and pour into a frosted cocktail glass then serve with a short straw.

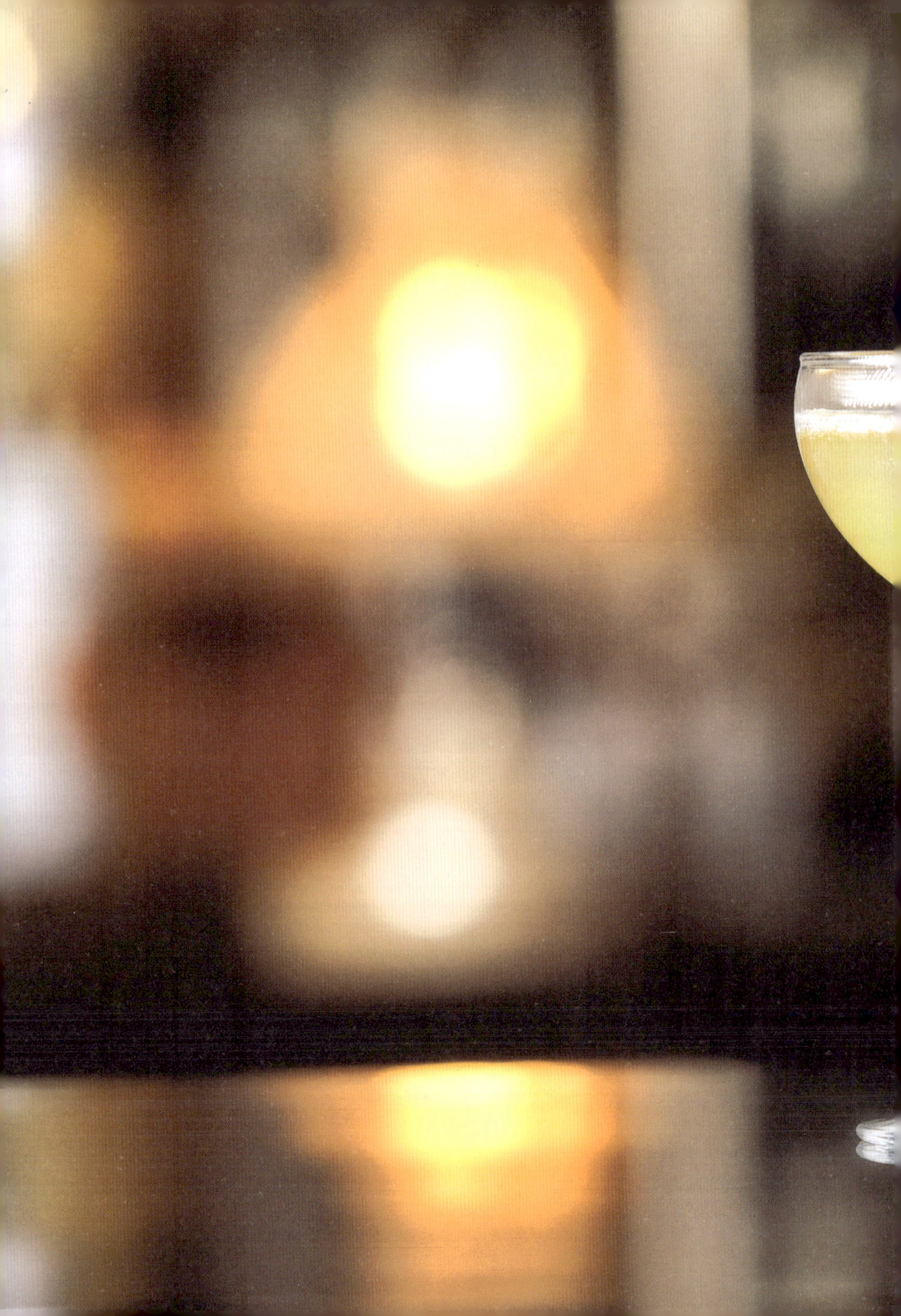

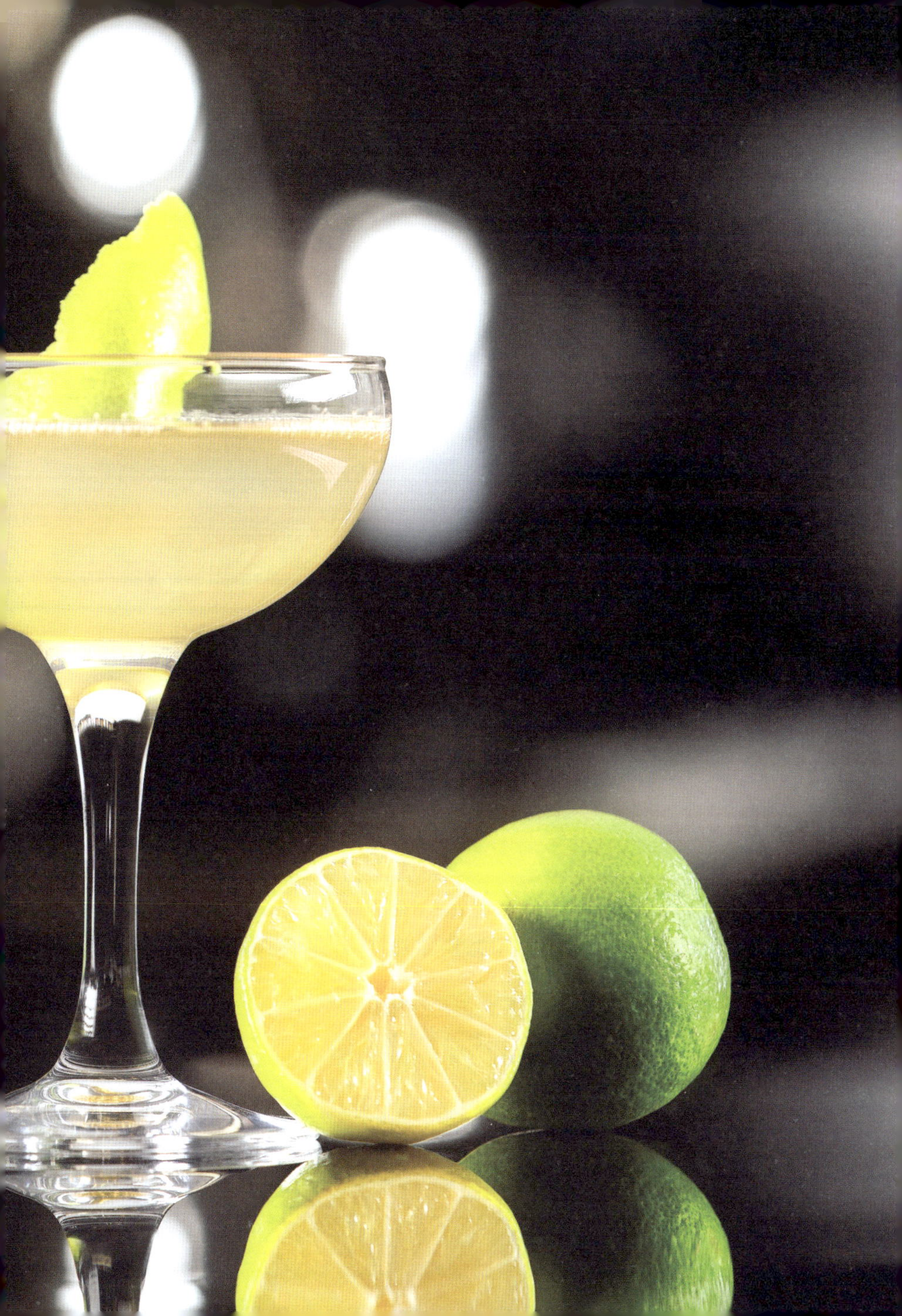

FROZEN STRAWBERRY DAIQUIRI

14.6% alc/vol
1.4 standard drinks

45 ml (1½ fl oz) Bacardi
2 dashes maraschino liqueur
15 ml (½ fl oz) fresh lime juice
15 ml (½ fl oz) thick cream (chilled)
1 teaspoon sugar syrup
4 fresh strawberries (diced)

Pour Bacardi, liqueur, juice, thick cream and sugar into a blender over a large amount of crushed ice then add diced strawberries. Blend until slushy and pour into a frosted cocktail glass then serve with a short red straw.

FROZEN MINT DAIQUIRI

30.4% alc/vol
1.8 standard drinks

60 ml (2 fl oz) Bacardi
10 ml (⅓ fl oz) fresh lime juice
1 teaspoon sugar syrup
6 fresh mint leaves

Pour Bacardi, juice and sugar into a blender over a large amount of crushed ice then add mint leaves. Blend until slushy and pour into a frosted cocktail glass then serve with a short green straw.

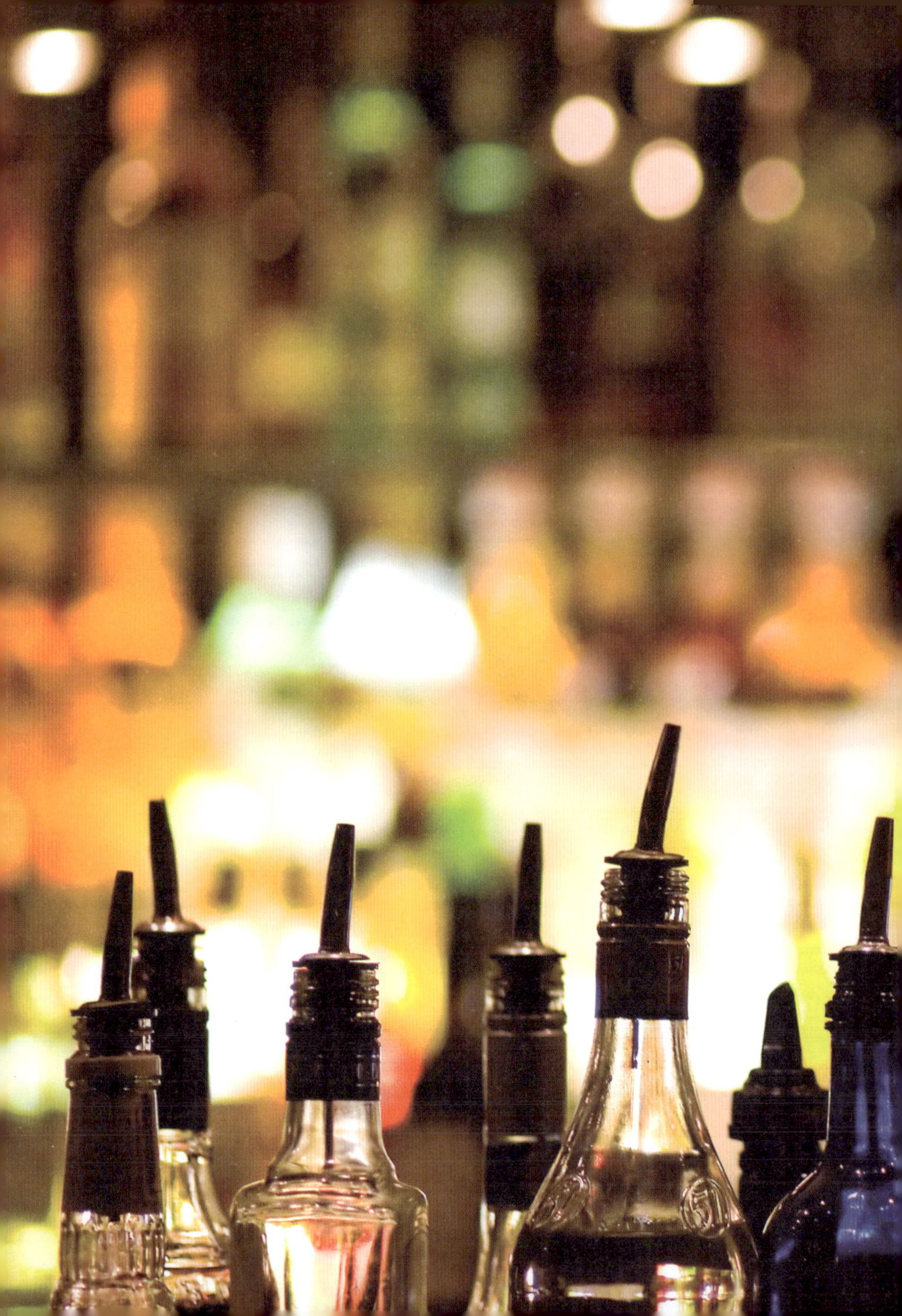

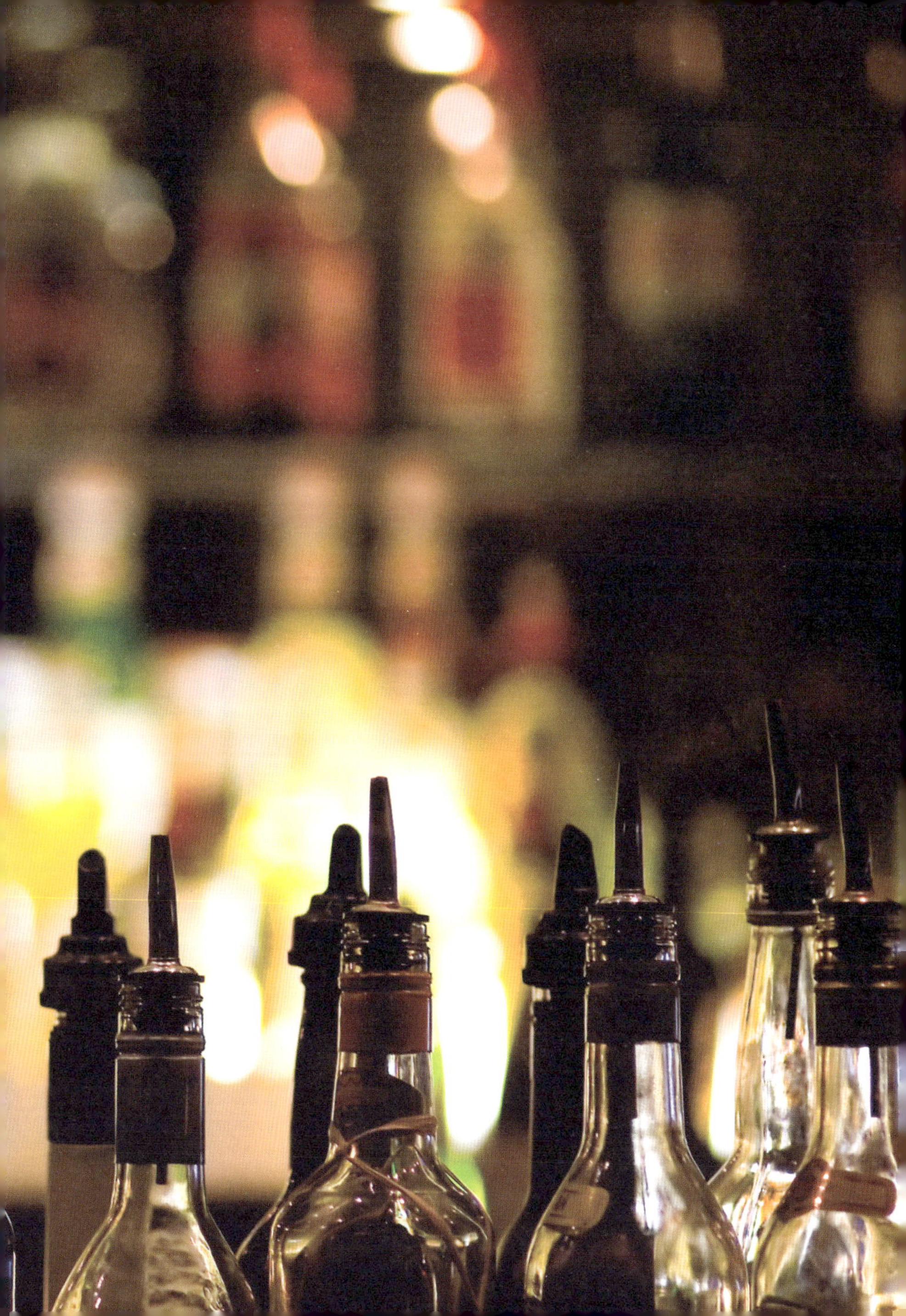

Glossary

% alc/vol

Amaretto Almond-flavored liqueur that originated from Italy in 1525....................... **28**

Amer Picon Bitter orange-flavored liqueur produced from quinine and spices. It is an apéritif liqueur originating from France. **25**

Apricot Brandy Apricot-flavored brandy............................ **23**

Bacardi Brand name of a light rum produced in Cuba. **37.5**

Banana Liqueur Banana-flavored liqueur........................ **23**

Chambord Black raspberry-flavored liqueur produced in the Burgundy region of France........................ **16.5**

Coconut Liqueur Coconut-flavored liqueur with a light rum-base........................ **23**

Cointreau Sweet orange-flavored liqueur that is colorless and arguably the world's finest Triple Sec. It has been produced by the Cointreau family in France since 1849........ **40**

Crème de Cassis Blackcurrant-flavored liqueur. **20**

Curaçao Sweet orange-flavored liqueur produced from curaçao orange peel. It is available in six varieties: blue, green, orange, red, white (clear) and yellow........................ **25**

Damiana Liqueur Light herbal-based liqueur produced in Mexico and created from the damiana herb........................ **30**

Galliano Aniseed and licorice-flavored liqueur with a distinctive yellow color. Produced in Italy from over 80 berries, herbs and roots. **35**

Ginger Brandy Ginger-flavored brandy with a light brown color. **35**

Grand Marnier Orange-flavored Cognac-based liqueur produced in France and created in 1880. It is available in two varieties: red ribbon and yellow ribbon – red ribbon has a higher % alc/vol at 40% alc/vol........................ **40**

Grenadine Sweet red syrup, flavored with pomegranate juice........................ **Nil**

Kahlúa Coffee-flavored liqueur that is produced in Mexico. **20**

Kirsch Clear bitter cherry-flavored brandy that can be added to cocktails to enhance the flavor of fruits. 37

Mango Liqueur Mango-flavored liqueur. 23

Maraschino Liqueur Cherry-flavored clear liqueur that originated in Italy. 40

Midori Brand name of a honeydew melon-flavored liqueur that is green in color and produced by the Suntory Distilling Company in Japan. 21

Parfait Amour Citrus and rose scented, violet colored liqueur. Produced from brandy, citrus and herbs, it originated from France. 23

Peach Liqueur Peach-flavored liqueur. 23

Rum (Dark) Spirit is aged in wooden barrels for between three and twelve years .... with the addition of caramel added in some cases to darken the spirit. Dark Rum varieties include Jamaican, Haitian and Martinique rums. 37

Rum (Light) Spirit aged for approximately six to twelve months in oak casks after being distilled in a column-still, which produces clear spirit. Originally produced in the southern Caribbean Islands. 38

Schnapps Generic name for flavored alcohol that is produced from grain or potato mash. Schnapps can be very sweet through to dry with many varieties available. % alc/vol content varies between the varieties. 20% alc/vol is average for commercial Schnapps. 20

Sherry Produced from grapes and fortified with brandy. True sherry originates from Jerez in southern Spain. 18

Spiced Rum Blended with a variety of spices. 35

Strawberry Daiquiri Mix .... Nil
Pre-prepared strawberry Daiquiri mix – just add Bacardi.

Strawberry Liqueur Strawberry-flavored liqueur. 23

Tia Maria Coffee-flavored rum-based Jamaican liqueur. 26.5

Vermouth (Dry) A Fortified wine-based apéritif produced from herbs, flowers and roots. 18

Vermouth (Sweet) 15

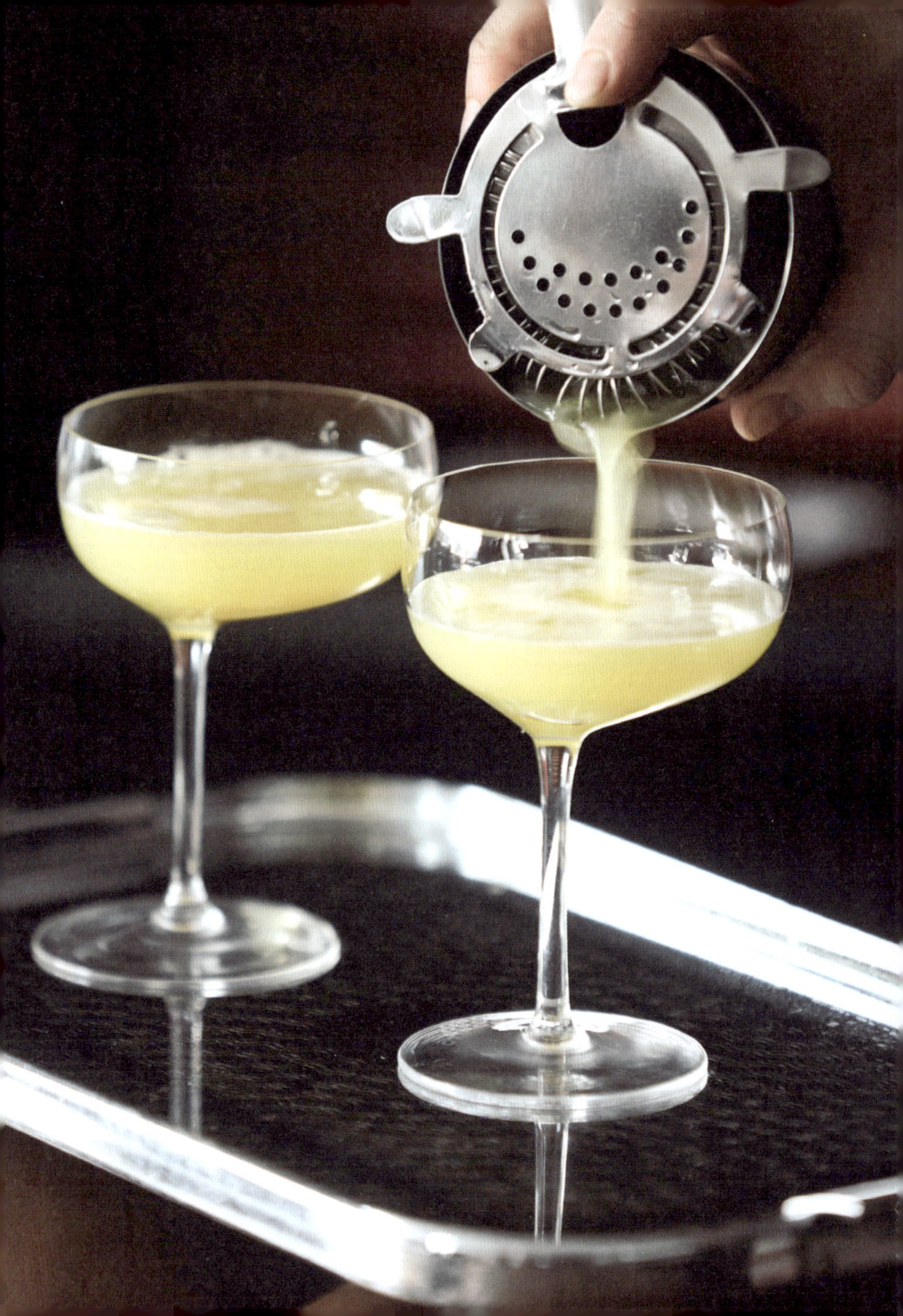

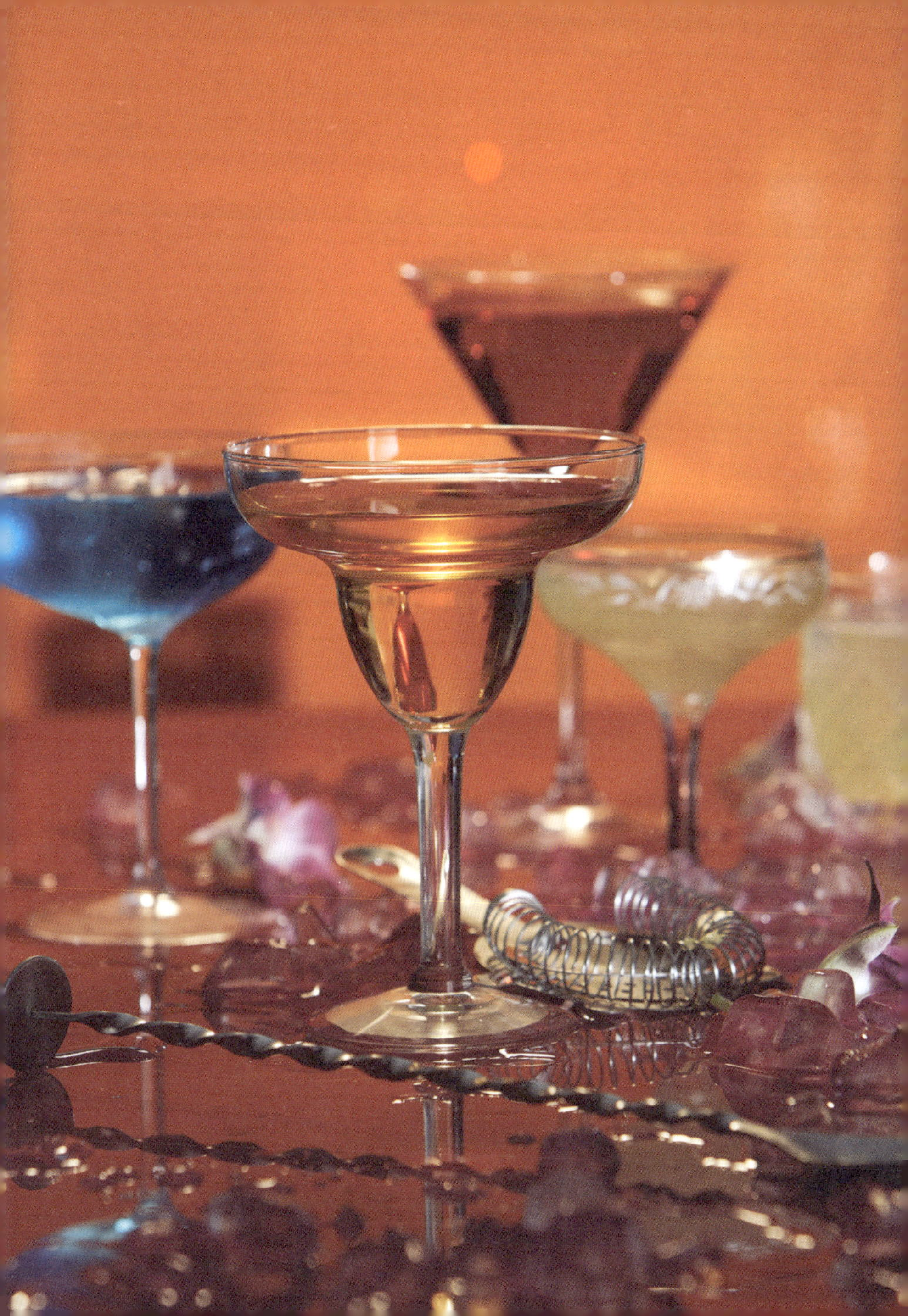

Index

A

Amaretto Colada 38
Apple Colada 33
Apple Daiquiri 111

B

Bacardi Daiquiri 62
Banana Colada 26
Banana Daiquiri 77
Banana Daiquiri No.2 88
Blueberry Daiquiri 94
Blue Colada 42

C

Chambord Daiquiri 89
Chamborlada 50
Cherry Daiquiri 71
Cocoa Colada 40
Coconut Daiquiri 113
Coffee Colada 36
Colada Collision 45

D

Daiquiri Blossom 75
Daiquiri Cocktail 98
Daiquiri Liberal 91
Daiquiri Nacional 78
Derby Daiquiri 79

F

French Daiquiri 112
Frozen Apple Daiquiri 117
Frozen Banana Daiquiri 123
Frozen Blue Daiquiri 70
Frozen Daiquiri 59
Frozen Guava Daiquiri 125
Frozen Guava-Orange Daiquiri 101
Frozen Mint Daiquiri 133
Frozen Passionfruit Daiquiri 124
Frozen Peach Daiquiri 126
Frozen Pineapple Daiquiri 121
Frozen Sesame Daiquiri 100
Frozen Sherry Daiquiri 128

Frozen Soursop Daiquiri 129
Frozen Strawberry Daiquiri 132

G
Galliano Daiquiri 60
Ginger Colada 25

K
King's Daiquiri 93
Kiwi Daiquiri 114

L
La Florida Daiquiri 85
Lime Daiquiri 105

M
Mandarin Daiquiri 116
Mango Daiquiri 68
Melon Colada 39

O
Orange Daiquiri 106

P
Passion Daiquiri 108
Patria Colada 35
Peach Daiquiri 82
Piña Colada 31
Pineapple Daiquiri 103

R
Raspberry Colada 34
Rockmelon Daiquiri 87

S
St. Martin Colada 44
Strawberry Banana Colada 47
Strawberry Colada 23
Strawberry Daiquiri 64

T
The All-American Daiquiri 61
Tropicolada 28

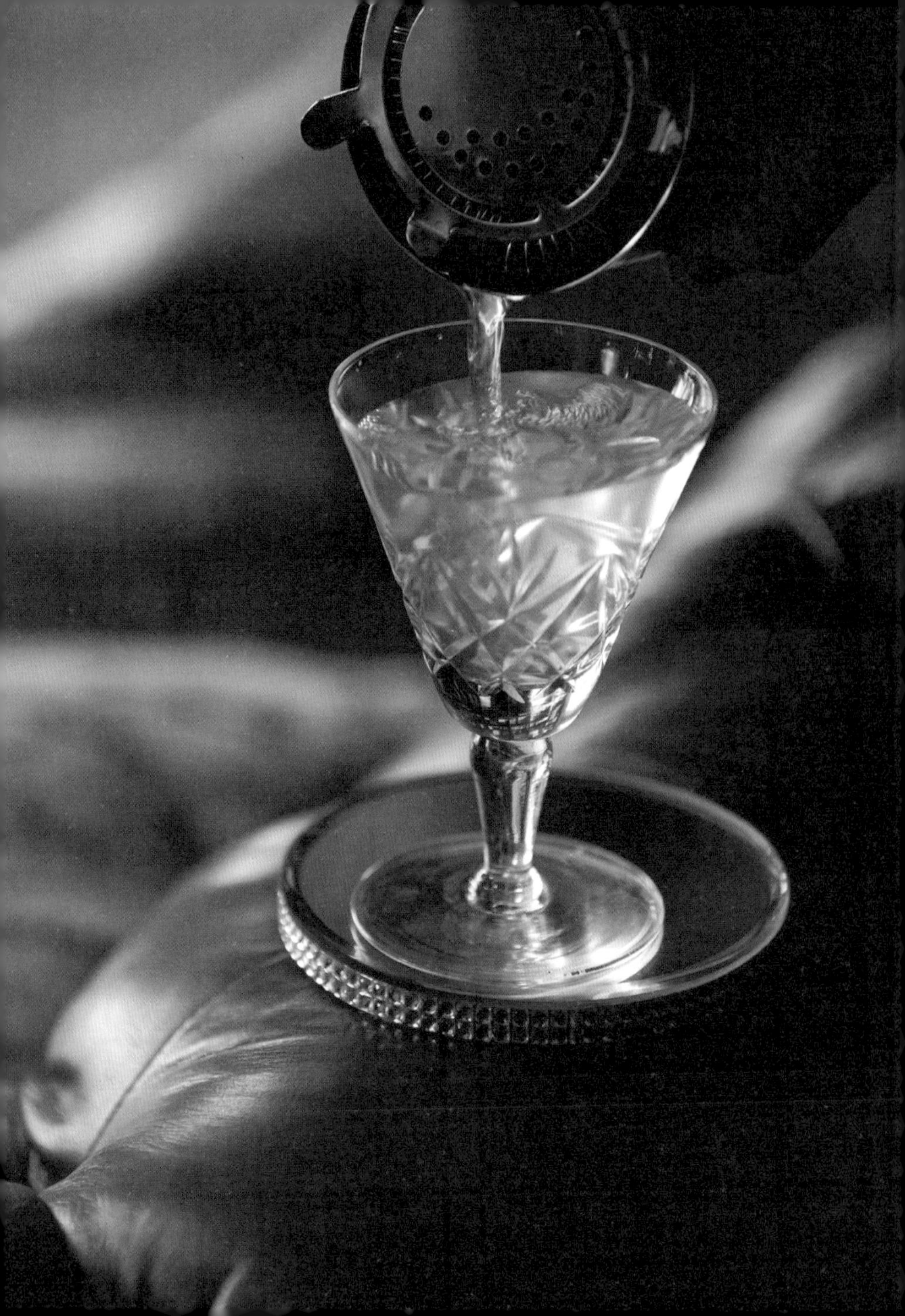

First published in 2017 by New Holland Publishers
London • Sydney • Auckland

The Chandlery 50 Westminster Bridge Road London SE1 7QY United Kingdom
1/66 Gibbes Street Chatswood NSW 2067 Australia
5/39 Woodside Ave Northcote Auckland 0627 New Zealand

www.newhollandpublishers.com

Copyright © 2017 New Holland Publishers
Copyright © 2017 in text: Steve Quirk
Copyright © 2017 in images: New Holland Publishers

All rights reserved. No part of this publication may be reproduced, stored in a retrieval system or transmitted, in any form or by any means, electronic, mechanical, photocopying, recording or otherwise, without the prior written permission of the publishers and copyright holders.

A record of this book is held at the British Library and the National Library of Australia.

ISBN 9781742579542

Group Managing Director: Fiona Schultz
Publisher: Alan Whiticker
Project Editor: Sarah Menary
Designer: Lorena Susak
Proof Reader: Kaitlyn Smith
Production Director: James Mills-Hicks
Special thanks to Chris Howley for making the cocktails
Printer: Hang Tai Printing Company Limited

10 9 8 7 6 5 4 3 2 1

Keep up with New Holland Publishers on Facebook
www.facebook.com/NewHollandPublishers